American Bible Society

The Gospel According to St. Matthew in English and Mandarin

American Bible Society

The Gospel According to St. Matthew in English and Mandarin

ISBN/EAN: 9783337280833

Printed in Europe, USA, Canada, Australia, Japan

Cover: Foto ©Lupo / pixelio.de

More available books at **www.hansebooks.com**

音福太馬

字西中

THE GOSPEL ACCORDING TO

ST. MATTHEW

IN

ENGLISH AND MANDARIN.

PUBLISHED BY THE

AMERICAN BIBLE SOCIETY.

SHANGHAI:
AMERICAN PRESBYTERIAN MISSION PRESS.

1899.

書音福傳太馬

THE GOSPEL ACCORDING TO MATTHEW.

CHAPTER 1.

THE book of the generation of Jesus Christ, the son of David, the son of Abraham.

2 Abraham begat Isaac; and Isaac begat Jacob; and Jacob begat Judas and his brethren;

3 And Judas begat Phares and Zara of Thamar; and Phares begat Esrom; and Esrom begat Aram;

4 And Aram begat Aminadab; and Aminadab begat Naasson; and Naasson begat Salmon;

5 And Salmon begat Booz of Rachab; and Booz begat Obed of Ruth; and Obed begat Jesse;

6 And Jesse begat David the king; and David the king begat Solomon of her *that had been the wife* of Urias;

7 And Solomon begat Roboam and Roboam begat Abia; and Abia begat Asa;

8 And Asa begat Josaphat; and Josaphat begat Joram; and Joram begat Ozias;

9 And Ozias begat Joatham; and Joatham begat Achaz; and Achaz begat Ezekias;

第一章

一亞伯拉罕的後裔、大衛的子孫、耶穌基督的家譜記在下面亞伯拉罕生以撒以撒生雅各雅各生猶大和猶大的弟兄猶大與大馬氏生法勒士同撒拉法勒士生以士崙以士崙生亞蘭亞蘭生亞米拏達亞米拏達生拏順拏順生撒捫撒捫娶喇合民生波士波士娶路得氏生阿伯阿伯生耶西耶西生大衛王大衛王娶烏利亞的妻子生所羅門所羅門生羅波喑羅波喑生亞比亞亞比亞生亞撒亞撒生約沙法約沙法生約蘭約生烏西亞烏西亞生約但約但生哈士亞哈士亞生希西家

ST. MATTHEW.

10 And Ezekias begat Manasses; and Manasses begat Amon; and Amon begat Josias;

11 And Josias begat Jechonias and his brethren, about the time they were carried away to Babylon:

12 And after they were brought to Babylon, Jechonias begat Salathiel; and Salathiel begat Zorobabel;

13 And Zorobabel begat Abiud; and Abiud begat Eliakim; and Eliakim begat Azor;

14 And Azor begat Sadoc; and Sadoc begat Achim; and Achim begat Eliud;

15 And Eliud begat Eleazar; and Eleazar begat Matthan; and Matthan begat Jacob;

16 And Jacob begat Joseph the husband of Mary, of whom was born Jesus, who is called Christ.

17 So all the generations from Abraham to David *are* fourteen generations; and from David until the carrying away into Babylon *are* fourteen generations; and from the carrying away into Babylon unto Christ *are* fourteen generations.

18 ¶ Now the birth of Jesus Christ was on this wise: When as his mother Mary was espoused to Joseph, before they came together, she was found with child of the Holy Ghost.

馬太第一章

希西家生瑪拏西、瑪拏西生亞們、亞們生約西亞、約西亞生耶哥尼亞和耶哥尼亞的弟兄、那時候百姓被遷到巴比倫去了、遷到巴比倫之後耶哥尼亞生撒拉鐵、撒拉鐵生所羅巴伯、所羅巴伯生亞比鬱、亞比鬱生以利亞金、以利亞金生亞所、亞所生撒督、撒督生亞金、亞金生以律、以律生以利亞撒、以利亞撒生馬但、馬但生雅各、雅各生約瑟、約瑟就是馬利亞的丈夫、馬利亞生稱呼基督的耶穌從亞伯拉罕到大衛共有十四代、從大衛到遷巴比倫共有十四代、從遷巴比倫到基督又有十四代。○耶穌基督降生的事、記在下面、他母親馬利亞被約瑟聘定為妻還未曾迎娶馬利亞受了聖靈的感動、有了身孕。

ST. MATTHEW.

19 Then Joseph her husband, being a just *man*, and not willing to make her a public example, was minded to put her away privily.

20 But while he thought on these things, behold, the angel of the Lord appeared unto him in a dream, saying, Joseph, thou son of David, fear not to take unto thee Mary thy wife: for that which is conceived in her is of the Holy Ghost.

21 And she shall bring forth a son, and thou shalt call his name JESUS: for he shall save his people from their sins.

22 Now all this was done, that it might be fulfilled which was spoken of the Lord by the prophet, saying,

23 Behold, a virgin shall be with child, and shall bring forth a son, and they shall call his name Emmanuel, which being interpreted is, God with us.

24 Then Joseph being raised from sleep did as the angel of the Lord had bidden him, and took unto him his wife:

25 And knew her not till she had brought forth her firstborn son: and he called his name JESUS.

馬太第一章

他丈夫約瑟是個義人、不肯明明的羞辱他、想要暗暗的將他休了正思念這事的時候夢見　主的使者來對他說、大衛的子孫約瑟你只管娶過你妻子馬利亞來、不用疑懼他有身孕是因爲受了　聖靈的感動他必要生一個兒子、你可以給他起名叫耶穌、因爲他要將他的百姓從罪惡裏救出來這事成就便應驗、或作爲要應驗　主託先知所說的話他說童女將要懷孕生子人將稱他的名爲以馬內利、繙出來就是　神在我們中間的意思約瑟醒了起來就遵著　主的使者所吩咐的將他妻子娶過來只是沒有和他同房等他生了頭一個兒子、就起名叫耶穌。

4 ST. MATTHEW.

CHAPTER 2.

NOW when Jesus was born in Bethlehem of Judea in the days of Herod the king, behold, there came wise men from the east to Jerusalem,

2 Saying, Where is he that is born King of the Jews? for we have seen his star in the east, and are come to worship him.

3 When Herod the king had heard *these things,* he was troubled, and all Jerusalem with him.

4 And when he had gathered all the chief priests and scribes of the people together, he demanded of them where Christ should be born.

5 And they said unto him, In Bethlehem of Judea: for thus it is written by the prophet,

6 And thou Bethlehem, *in* the land of Juda, art not the least among the princes of Juda: for out of thee shall come a Governor, that shall rule my people Israel.

7 Then Herod, when he had privily called the wise men, inquired of them diligently what time the star appeared.

馬太第二章

第二章

當希律王的時候耶穌生在猶太的伯利恆有幾個博士從東方來到耶路撒冷說、

那剛纔生的猶太人的王在那裏我們在東方看見他的星特來拜他希律王聽見的話就慌了耶路撒冷合城的人也都慌了、

就召了衆祭司長和民間讀書人來、問他們說基督當生在何處、他們回答說應當生在猶太的伯利恆因爲有先知記的話說猶太的伯利恆阿你在猶太的府縣裏並不是最小的將來有一位君王從你那裏出來、牧養我以色列民當下希律暗暗的召了博士來、細問那星出現的時

ST. MATTHEW.

8 And he sent them to Bethlehem, and said, Go and search diligently for the young child; and when ye have found *him*, bring me word again, that I may come and worship him also.

9 When they had heard the king, they departed; and, lo, the star, which they saw in the east, went before them, till it came and stood over where the young child was.

10 When they saw the star, they rejoiced with exceeding great joy.

11 ¶ And when they were come into the house, they saw the young child with Mary his mother, and fell down, and worshipped him: and when they had opened their treasures, they presented unto him gifts; gold, and frankincense, and myrrh.

12 And being warned of God in a dream that they should not return to Herod, they departed into their own country another way.

13 And when they were departed, behold, the angel of the Lord appeareth to Joseph in a dream, saying, Arise, and take the young child and his mother, and flee into Egypt, and be thou there until I bring thee word: for Herod will seek the young child to destroy him.

14 When he arose, he took the young child and his mother by night, and departed into Egypt:

就差遣他們往伯利恆去、對他們說你們去仔細尋訪那嬰孩、遇見他、就來報信與我、我也去拜他、博士領命去了、那東方所看見的星、忽然在前引路、直到嬰孩的地方、就停住在上頭、博士看見那星大大歡喜、進了房子、看見嬰孩和他母親馬利亞、就俯伏拜那嬰孩、揭開寶盒獻上黃金乳香沒藥爲禮物、博士因主在夢中指示他們不要回去見希律就從別的路上回本地去了、○他們去後約瑟夢見主的使者來對他說起來、帶著嬰孩同他母親逃往伊及去、在那裏住等我吩咐你、因爲希律要尋找嬰孩將他殺了、約瑟就起來、夜間帶著嬰孩同他母親逃往伊及

ST. MATTHEW.

15 And was there until the death of Herod: that it might be fulfilled which was spoken of the Lord by the prophet, saying, Out of Egypt have I called my son.

16 ¶ Then Herod, when he saw that he was mocked of the wise men, was exceeding wroth, and sent forth, and slew all the children that were in Bethlehem, and in all the coasts thereof, from two years old and under, according to the time which he had diligently inquired of the wise men.

17 Then was fulfilled that which was spoken by Jeremy the prophet, saying,

18 In Rama was there a voice heard, lamentation, and weeping, and great mourning, Rachel weeping *for* her children, and would not be comforted, because they are not.

19 ¶ But when Herod was dead, behold, an angel of the Lord appeareth in a dream to Joseph in Egypt,

20 Saying, Arise, and take the young child and his mother, and go into the land of Israel: for they are dead which sought the young child's life.

21 And he arose, and took the young child and his mother, and came into the land of Israel.

馬太第二章

住在那裏、直到希律死的時候、這就應驗　主託先知所說我從伊及召我兒子出來的話了十六希律自己是被博士愚弄就大怒差遣人將伯利恆城裏並四境所有的嬰孩照著他向博士所詳細查問的時候凡兩歲以裏的都殺盡了這正應驗先知耶利米的話說十八在拉馬聽見悲傷哀痛號哭的聲音是拉結氏哭他兒子不肯受安慰因為他兒子都不在了希律死後約瑟在伊及夢見　主的使者來對他說起來帶著嬰孩同他母親回以色列地方去因為要害嬰孩性命的人已經死了約瑟就起來帶著嬰孩同他母親往以色列地方去

ST. MATTHEW.

22 But when he heard that Archelaus did reign in Judea in the room of his father Herod, he was afraid to go thither: notwithstanding, being warned of God in a dream, he turned aside into the parts of Galilee:

23 And he came and dwelt in a city called Nazareth: that it might be fulfilled which was spoken by the prophets, He shall be called a Nazarene.

CHAPTER 3.

IN those days came John the Baptist, preaching in the wilderness of Judea,

2 And saying, Repent ye: for the kingdom of heaven is at hand.

3 For this is he that was spoken of by the prophet Esaias, saying, The voice of one crying in the wilderness, Prepare ye the way of the Lord, make his paths straight.

4 And the same John had his raiment of camel's hair, and a leathern girdle about his loins; and his meat was locusts and wild honey.

5 Then went out to him Jerusalem, and all Judea, and all the region round about Jordan,

6 And were baptized of him in Jordan, confessing their sins.

馬太第三章

只因聽見亞基老接著他父親希律作了猶太王、就懼怕不敢往那裏去、在夢中蒙主指示、便往加利利境內去了、到了一個地方名叫拏撒勒、就住在那裏這正應驗先知所說人將稱他為拏撒勒人的話了。

第三章

那時有施洗的約翰、在猶太曠野講道說天國近了、你們應當悔改。這人就是先知以賽亞所指著說的、他說在曠野有人聲喊叫說豫備 主的道修直了 主的路。

約翰穿駱駝毛的衣服、腰繫皮帶喫的是蝗蟲野蜜那時候耶路撒冷猶太全地、和約但河兩邊的人、都出去到約翰那裏承認自己的罪惡、在約但河裏受他的洗。

8 ST. MATTHEW.

7 ¶ But when he saw many of the Pharisees and Sadducees come to his baptism, he said unto them, O generation of vipers, who hath warned you to flee from the wrath to come?

8 Bring forth therefore fruits meet for repentance:

9 And think not to say within yourselves, We have Abraham to *our* father: for I say unto you, that God is able of these stones to raise up children unto Abraham.

10 And now also the axe is laid unto the root of the trees: therefore every tree which bringeth not forth good fruit is hewn down, and cast into the fire.

11 I indeed baptize you with water unto repentance: but he that cometh after me is mightier than I, whose shoes I am not worthy to bear: he shall baptize you with the Holy Ghost, and *with* fire:

12 Whose fan *is* in his hand, and he will thoroughly purge his floor, and gather his wheat into the garner; but he will burn up the chaff with unquenchable fire.

13 ¶ Then cometh Jesus from Galilee to Jordan unto John, to be baptized of him.

14 But John forbade him, saying, I have need to be baptized of thee, and comest thou to me?

馬太第三章

約翰見許多法利賽人、撒都該人、也到他這裏來受洗、就對他們說、毒蛇一類的、誰告訴你們躲避將來的刑罰呢、你們應當結善果表明悔改的心、不要自己心裏說、亞伯拉罕是我們的祖宗我對你們說、神能叫這些石頭、做亞伯拉罕的子孫、如今斧子已經放在樹根上、凡不結好果子的樹、就砍下來、丟在火裏、我是用水施洗、叫你們悔改、但那在我以後來的、能力比我更大、我與他提鞵、也是不配的、他將用聖靈和火與你們施洗、他手挈著簸箕、要簸淨了場上的麥子、將麥子收在倉裏、將穅用不滅的火燒了、○那時候耶穌從加利利到了約但河、來見約翰要受他的洗。約翰推辭說、我當受你的洗、你倒就了我來麼、

15 And Jesus answering said unto him, Suffer *it to be so* now: for thus it becometh us to fulfil all righteousness. Then he suffered him.

16 And Jesus, when he was baptized, went up straightway out of the water: and, lo, the heavens were opened unto him, and he saw the Spirit of God descending like a dove, and lighting upon him:

17 And lo a voice from heaven, saying, This is my beloved Son, in whom I am well pleased.

CHAPTER 4.

THEN was Jesus led up of the Spirit into the wilderness to be tempted of the devil.

2 And when he had fasted forty days and forty nights, he was afterward a hungered.

3 And when the tempter came to him, he said, If thou be the Son of God, command that these stones be made bread.

4 But he answered and said, It is written, Man shall not live by bread alone, but by every word that proceedeth out of the mouth of God.

5 Then the devil taketh him up into the holy city, and setteth him on a pinnacle of the temple,

ST. MATTHEW.

6 And saith unto him, If thou be the Son of God, cast thyself down: for it is written, He shall give his angels charge concerning thee: and in *their* hands they shall bear thee up, lest at any time thou dash thy foot against a stone.

7 Jesus said unto him, It is written again, Thou shalt not tempt the Lord thy God.

8 Again, the devil taketh him up into an exceeding high mountain, and sheweth him all the kingdoms of the world, and the glory of them;

9 And saith unto him, All these things will I give thee, if thou wilt fall down and worship me.

10 Then saith Jesus unto him, Get thee hence, Satan: for it is written, Thou shalt worship the Lord thy God, and him only shalt thou serve.

11 Then the devil leaveth him, and, behold, angels came and ministered unto him.

12 ¶ Now when Jesus had heard that John was cast into prison, he departed into Galilee;

13 And leaving Nazareth, he came and dwelt in Capernaum, which is upon the sea coast, in the borders of Zabulon and Nephthalim:

14 That it might be fulfilled which was spoken by Esaias the prophet, saying,

馬太第四章

對他說、你若是 神的兒子、可以跳下去、經上說、主盼附天使用手扶持你、免得你的腳撞在石頭上、耶穌說經上又說、不可試探 主你的 神。魔鬼又領他上最高的山將天下的萬國和萬國的榮華、指給他看、說你若俯伏拜我、我就將這一切都給你、耶穌說、撒但退下去、經上說應當拜 主你的 神、單要奉事他。於是魔鬼離了耶穌、天使來服事他。○耶穌聽見約翰下了監、就往加利利去、後又離開拏撒勒往迦百農去、就住在那裏那地方靠海在西布倫納大利的境內、就應了先知以賽亞所說的話、

ST. MATTHEW.

15 The land of Zabulon, and the land of Nephthalim, *by* the way of the sea, beyond Jordan, Galilee of the Gentiles;

16 The people which sat in darkness saw great light; and to them which sat in the region and shadow of death light is sprung up.

17 ¶ From that time Jesus began to preach, and to say, Repent: for the kingdom of heaven is at hand.

18 ¶ And Jesus, walking by the sea of Galilee, saw two brethren, Simon called Peter, and Andrew his brother, casting a net into the sea: for they were fishers.

19 And he saith unto them, Follow me, and I will make you fishers of men.

20 And they straightway left *their* nets, and followed him.

21 And going on from thence, he saw other two brethren, James *the son* of Zebedee, and John his brother, in a ship with Zebedee their father, mending their nets; and he called them.

22 And they immediately left the ship and their father, and followed him.

23 ¶ And Jesus went about all Galilee, teaching in their synagogues, and preaching the gospel of the kingdom, and healing all manner of sickness and all manner of disease among the people.

馬太第四章

十五 他說沿海靠近約但河的西布倫納大利外邦人所居住的加利利那地方住在黑暗裏的百姓看見大光照耀他們○從這時候耶穌講道說天國近了你們應當悔改。耶穌在加利利海邊行走看見兄弟二人就是西門稱呼彼得的和他兄弟安得烈在海裏撒網他們本是打魚的人。耶穌對他們說來跟從我我要叫你們得人如得魚一樣他們就丟下網跟從了耶穌。又看見兄弟二人就是西庇太的兒子雅各和雅各的兄弟約翰同他父親在船上補網耶穌招呼他們。他們立刻離了船別了父親跟從了耶穌。○耶穌走遍加利利在各處會堂教訓人、宣講天國的福音醫治百姓各樣的疾病疼痛。

24 And his fame went throughout all Syria: and they brought unto him all sick people that were taken with divers diseases and torments, and those which were possessed with devils, and those which were lunatic, and those that had the palsy; and he healed them.

25 And there followed him great multitudes of people from Galilee, and *from* Decapolis, and *from* Jerusalem, and *from* Judea, and *from* beyond Jordan

CHAPTER 5.

AND seeing the multitudes, he went up into a mountain: and when he was set, his disciples came unto him:

2 And he opened his mouth, and taught them, saying,

3 Blessed *are* the poor in spirit: for theirs is the kingdom of heaven.

4 Blessed *are* they that mourn: for they shall be comforted.

5 Blessed *are* the meek: for they shall inherit the earth.

6 Blessed *are* they which do hunger and thirst after righteousness: for they shall be filled.

7 Blessed *are* the merciful: for they shall obtain mercy.

他的聲名傳遍了敘利亞地方有人帶著患各樣病痛的人、和被鬼附的、顛狂的、癱瘋的、到耶穌面前來耶穌都醫好他們、當下有許多人從加利利低加波利耶路撒冷猶太約但河外邊來跟從耶穌、

第五章

一耶穌看見這許多人、就上山坐下、門徒進前來、二耶穌開口教訓他們說、三虛心的人是有福的、因為天國就是他們的國、四哀慟的人是有福的、因為他們必要受安慰、五柔和的人是有福的、因為他們必要得地土、六羨慕仁義如飢如渴的人是有福的、因為他們必要得飽、七憐恤人的人是有福的、因為他們必要蒙憐恤、

ST. MATTHEW.

8 Blessed *are* the pure in heart: for they shall see God.

9 Blessed *are* the peacemakers: for they shall be called the children of God.

10 Blessed *are* they which are persecuted for righteousness' sake: for theirs is the kingdom of heaven.

11 Blessed are ye, when *men* shall revile you, and persecute *you*, and shall say all manner of evil against you falsely, for my sake.

12 Rejoice, and be exceeding glad: for great *is* your reward in heaven: for so persecuted they the prophets which were before you.

13 ¶ Ye are the salt of the earth: but if the salt have lost his savour, wherewith shall it be salted? it is thenceforth good for nothing, but to be cast out, and to be trodden under foot of men.

14 Ye are the light of the world. A city that is set on a hill cannot be hid.

15 Neither do men light a candle, and put it under a bushel, but on a candlestick; and it giveth light unto all that are in the house.

16 Let your light so shine before men, that they may see your good works, and glorify your Father which is in heaven.

馬太第五章

清心的人是有福的、因為他們必要得見　神。

和睦的人是有福的、因為他們必要稱為　神的兒子。

為義受逼迫的人是有福的、因為天國就是他們的國。

人若因為我辱罵你們、逼迫你們、造各樣惡言毀謗你們、你們就有福了。應當歡喜快樂、因為你們在天上的賞賜是大的、在你們以前的先知也是這樣被人逼迫。○你們是世上的鹽、鹽若失了味、如何能再鹹呢、以後無用、不過丟在外面被人踐踏了。你們是世上的光、城造在山上、是不能隱藏的。人點燈不放在斗底下、放在燈臺上、就照耀一家的人、你們的光、也當這樣照在人前、叫人看見你們的好行為、就將榮耀歸與你們在天上的父。

17 ¶ Think not that I am come to destroy the law, or the prophets: I am not come to destroy, but to fulfil.

18 For verily I say unto you, Till heaven and earth pass, one jot or one tittle shall in no wise pass from the law, till all be fulfilled.

19 Whosoever therefore shall break one of these least commandments, and shall teach men so, he shall be called the least in the kingdom of heaven: but whosoever shall do and teach *them*, the same shall be called great in the kingdom of heaven.

20 For I say unto you, That except your righteousness shall exceed *the righteousness* of the scribes and Pharisees, ye shall in no case enter into the kingdom of heaven.

21 ¶ Ye have heard that it was said by them of old time, Thou shalt not kill; and whosoever shall kill shall be in danger of the judgment:

22 But I say unto you, That whosoever is angry with his brother without a cause shall be in danger of the judgment: and whosoever shall say to his brother, Raca, shall be in danger of the council: but whosoever shall say, Thou fool, shall be in danger of hell fire.

23 Therefore if thou bring thy gift to the altar, and there rememberest that thy brother hath aught against thee;

○不要想我來、是要廢掉律法和先知的道理、我來、不是要廢掉、正是要成全我實在告訴你們、等到天地都沒有了律法的一點一畫也不能廢掉這誡命裏最小的一條又教訓人這樣、他在天國就算爲最小的人若遵行這誡命又教訓人遵行、他在天國就算爲大的、我告訴你們你們的善行若不比讀書人和法利賽人的善行更大、斷不能進入天國○你們聽見有吩咐古人的話說不可殺人凡殺人的必當受刑只是我告訴你們人若無緣無故向兄弟動怒也必當受刑若罵兄弟是拉加就當送到公堂裏罵兄弟是魔利就當下在地獄的火裏、拉加冤利皆是罵話所以你要在祭壇上獻禮物想起你得罪了兄弟、

ST. MATTHEW.

24 Leave there thy gift before the altar, and go thy way; first be reconciled to thy brother, and then come and offer thy gift.

25 Agree with thine adversary quickly, while thou art in the way with him; lest at any time the adversary deliver thee to the judge, and the judge deliver thee to the officer, and thou be cast into prison.

26 Verily I say unto thee, Thou shalt by no means come out thence, till thou hast paid the uttermost farthing.

27 ¶ Ye have heard that it was said by them of old time, Thou shalt not commit adultery:

28 But I say unto you, That whosoever looketh on a woman to lust after her hath committed adultery with her already in his heart.

29 And if thy right eye offend thee, pluck it out, and cast *it* from thee: for it is profitable for thee that one of thy members should perish, and not *that* thy whole body should be cast into hell.

30 And if thy right hand offend thee, cut it off, and cast *it* from thee: for it is profitable for thee that one of thy members should perish, and not *that* thy whole body should be cast into hell.

31 It hath been said, Whosoever shall put away his wife, let him give her a writing of divorcement:

馬太第五章

就將禮物留在壇前、先去同兄弟和好了、然後來獻你的禮物、有人要告你、你還同他在道路上就趕緊與他和息恐怕他送你到官、官交給衙役將你收監、我實在告訴你、你若有一分一毫未曾還清萬不能從那裏出來、○你們聽見吩咐古人的話說、不可姦淫、只是我告訴你們、凡看見婦女就動淫念的、這人心裏已經姦淫了、若是右眼叫你犯罪、就剜出來丟掉、寗可失去百體中的一體、免得全身被丟在地獄裏、若是右手叫你犯罪、就砍下來丟掉、寗可失去百體中的一體、免得全身被丟在地獄裏、○又有話說、人若休妻、就當給他休書、

32 But I say unto you, That whosoever shall put away his wife, saving for the cause of fornication, causeth her to commit adultery: and whosoever shall marry her that is divorced committeth adultery.

33 ¶ Again, ye have heard that it hath been said by them of old time, Thou shalt not forswear thyself, but shalt perform unto the Lord thine oaths:

34 But I say unto you, Swear not at all; neither by heaven; for it is God's throne:

35 Nor by the earth; for it is his footstool: neither by Jerusalem; for it is the city of the great King.

36 Neither shall thou swear by the head, because thou canst not make one hair white or black.

37 But let your communication be, Yea, yea; Nay, nay: for whatsoever is more than these cometh of evil.

38 ¶ Ye have heard that it hath been said, An eye for an eye, and a tooth for a tooth:

39 But I say unto you, That ye resist not evil: but whosoever shall smite thee on thy right cheek, turn to him the other also.

40 And if any man will sue thee at the law, and take away thy coat, let him have *thy* cloak also.

ST. MATTHEW.

41 And whosoever shall compel thee to go a mile, go with him twain.
42 Give to him that asketh thee, and from him that would borrow of thee turn not thou away.
43 ¶ Ye have heard that it hath been said, Thou shalt love thy neighbour, and hate thine enemy.
44 But I say unto you, Love your enemies, bless them that curse you, do good to them that hate you, and pray for them which despitefully use you, and persecute you;
45 That ye may be the children of your Father which is in heaven: for he maketh his sun to rise on the evil and on the good, and sendeth rain on the just and on the unjust.
46 For if ye love them which love you, what reward have ye? do not even the publicans the same?
47 And if ye salute your brethren only, what do ye more *than others*? do not even the publicans so?
48 Be ye therefore perfect, even as your Father which is in heaven is perfect.

CHAPTER 6.

TAKE heed that ye do not your alms before men, to be seen of them: otherwise ye have no reward of your Father which is in heaven.

有人勉強你走一里地你就同他走二里地。有求你的就給他有向你借貸的不可推辭〇你們聽見有話說當愛你的朋友恨你們的仇敵只是我告訴你們要愛你們的仇敵倒要愛他祝福你們的咒詛你們的倒要爲他祈禱恨你們的倒要待他好毀謗你們逼迫你們的倒要爲他禱告如此就可以作你天父的兒子因爲天父叫日頭照好人也照歹人降雨給善人也給惡人你們單愛那愛你們的人還能有甚麼賞賜呢稅吏不也是這樣麼你們單請你兄弟的安有甚麼比人強的呢稅吏不也是這樣麼所以你們應當完全像你們在天上的父完全一樣。

第六章〇你們要小心不可在人面前施捨故意叫人看見若是這樣就不能得你天父的賞賜了。

18 ST. MATTHEW.

2 Therefore when thou doest *thine* alms, do not sound a trumpet before thee, as the hypocrites do in the synagogues and in the streets, that they may have glory of men. Verily I say unto you, They have their reward.

3 But when thou doest alms, let not thy left hand know what thy right hand doeth:

4 That thine alms may be in secret: and thy Father which seeth in secret himself shall reward thee openly.

5 ¶ And when thou prayest, thou shalt not be as the hypocrites *are:* for they love to pray standing in the synagogues and in the corners of the streets, that they may be seen of men. Verily I say unto you, They have their reward.

6 But thou, when thou prayest, enter into thy closet, and when thou hast shut thy door, pray to the Father which is in secret; and thy Father which seeth in secret shall reward thee openly.

7 But when ye pray, use not vain repetitions, as the heathen *do:* for they think that they shall be heard for their much speaking.

8 Be not ye therefore like unto them: for your Father knoweth what things ye have need of before ye ask him.

馬太第六章

二 所以你施捨的時候、不可在人面前吹號筒像那假冒為善的人、在會堂裏和街市上所行的、要人誇獎他我實在告訴你們、他們已經得了賞賜。三 你施捨的時候、不要叫左手知道右手所作的、總要在暗中作、你父在暗中察看、必在明處報應你。○ 你禱告的時候、不可像那假冒為善的人、喜歡站在會堂裏和十字路口上禱告故意叫人看見我實在告訴你們他們已經得了賞賜了、你要禱告當進嚴密的屋子裏關上門、禱告你在暗中的父你父在暗中察看必在明處報應你。你們禱告、不可像外邦人、說許多重複話、他們以為話多了必蒙應允你們不可效法他們因為沒有禱告之先你們所需用的你們的父已經知道了。

ST. MATTHEW.

9 After this manner therefore pray ye: Our Father which art in heaven, Hallowed be thy name.

10 Thy kingdom come. Thy will be done in earth, as *it is* in heaven.

11 Give us this day our daily bread.

12 And forgive us our debts, as we forgive our debtors.

13 And lead us not into temptation, but deliver us from evil: For thine is the kingdom, and the power, and the glory, for ever. Amen.

14 For if we forgive men their trespasses, your heavenly Father will also forgive you:

15 But if ye forgive not men their trespasses, neither will your Father forgive your trespasses.

16 ¶ Moreover when ye fast, be not, as the hypocrites, of a sad countenance: for they disfigure their faces, that they may appear unto men to fast. Verily I say unto you, They have their reward.

17 But thou, when thou fastest, anoint thine head, and wash thy face;

18 That thou appear not unto men to fast, but unto thy Father which is in secret: and thy Father which seeth in secret shall reward thee openly.

馬太第六章

你們禱告應當這樣說、我們在天上的父、願人都尊你的名爲聖、願你的國降臨、願你的旨意行在地上、如同行在天上、我們日用的飲食今日賜給我們、免了我們的債、如同我們免了人的債、不叫我們遇見試探、救我們脫離凶惡、因爲國度權柄榮耀全是你的、世世無窮、阿們、你們饒恕人的過犯、天父也饒恕你們的過犯○你們禁食的時候、不可像那假冒爲善的人、臉上帶著愁容、他們故意叫人看出他們禁食我實在告訴你們、他們已經得了賞賜了、你禁食應當梳頭洗臉、不要叫人看出你禁食、要叫暗中的父看見你父在暗中察看必在明處報應你、

19 ¶ Lay not up for yourselves treasures upon earth, where moth and rust doth corrupt, and where thieves break through and steal:
20 But lay up for yourselves treasures in heaven, where neither moth nor rust doth corrupt, and where thieves do not break through nor steal:
21 For where your treasure is, there will your heart be also.
22 The light of the body is the eye: if therefore thine eye be single, thy whole body shall be full of light.
23 But if thine eye be evil, thy whole body shall be full of darkness. If therefore the light that is in thee be darkness, how great is that darkness!
24 ¶ No man can serve two masters: for either he will hate the one, and love the other; or else he will hold to the one, and despise the other. Ye cannot serve God and mammon.
25 Therefore I say unto you, Take no thought for your life, what ye shall eat, or what ye shall drink; nor yet for your body, what ye shall put on. Is not the life more than meat, and the body than raiment?
26 Behold the fowls of the air: for they sow not, neither do they reap, nor gather into barns; yet your heavenly Father feedeth them. Are ye not much better than they?

○不要積蓄財寶在地上、地上有蟲子蛀、能銹壞、也有賊挖洞來偷、只要積蓄財寶在天上、天上沒有蟲子蛀、不能銹壞也沒有賊挖洞來偷、因爲你們的財寶在那裏、你們的心也在那裏。○眼睛就是身上的燈、眼睛瞭亮、全身都光明、眼睛昏花全身都黑暗、你裏頭的光若是黑暗、那黑暗就甚大了。○一個人不能事奉兩個主、或是惡這個愛那個、或是重這個輕那個、你們不能又事奉　神又事奉瑪門。瑪門卽財利之意、所以我告訴你們、不要爲生命憂慮喫甚麼喝甚麼、爲身體憂慮穿甚麼生命不比飲食貴重麼、身體不比衣裳貴重麼、你看空中的雀鳥也不種也不收也不積蓄在倉裏你們天父尚且養活他你們不比雀鳥貴重得多麼。

ST. MATTHEW.　　馬太第六章　21

27 Which of you by taking thought can add one cubit unto his stature?

28 And why take ye thought for raiment? Consider the lilies of the field, how they grow; they toil not, neither do they spin.

29 And yet I say unto you, That even Solomon in all his glory was not arrayed like one of these.

30 Wherefore, if God so clothe the grass of the field, which to day is, and to morrow is cast into the oven, *shall he* not much more *clothe* you, O ye of little faith?

31 Therefore take no thought, saying, What shall we eat? or, What shall we drink? or, Wherewithal shall we be clothed?

32 (For after all these things do the Gentiles seek:) for your heavenly Father knoweth that ye have need of all these things.

33 But seek ye first the kingdom of God, and his righteousness; and all these things shall be added unto you.

34 Take therefore no thought for the morrow: for the morrow shall take thought for the things of itself. Sufficient unto the day *is* the evil thereof.

你們裏頭、誰能用思慮多加一刻生命呢。你何必爲衣服憂慮呢、你看野地裏的百合花怎麼長起來這花也不勞苦也不織紡然而我告訴你們、就是所羅門極榮華的時候、他所穿戴的、還不如這花一朵呢。你們這小信的人、野地裏的草今日還在、明日就丟在爐裏。神還叫他有這樣的妝飾何況你們呢。所以不要憂慮說、喫甚麼喝甚麼穿甚麼這都是外邦人所求的、你們需用這些物、你們在天上的父、已經知道了你們須要先求　神的國和他的義天父自然將這些東西、加給你們了。所以不要爲明日憂慮明日的事、明日憂慮、一日只受一日的勞苦就彀了。

CHAPTER 7.

JUDGE not, that ye be not judged.

2 For with what judgment ye judge, ye shall be judged: and with what measure ye mete, it shall be measured to you again.

3 And why beholdest thou the mote that is in thy brother's eye, but considerest not the beam that is in thine own eye?

4 Or how wilt thou say to thy brother, Let me pull out the mote out of thine eye; and, behold, a beam is in thine own eye?

5 Thou hypocrite, first cast out the beam out of thine own eye; and then shalt thou see clearly to cast out the mote out of thy brother's eye.

6 ¶ Give not that which is holy unto the dogs, neither cast ye your pearls before swine, lest they trample them under their feet, and turn again and rend you.

7 ¶ Ask, and it shall be given you; seek, and ye shall find; knock, and it shall be opened unto you;

8 For every one that asketh receiveth; and he that seeketh findeth; and to him that knocketh it shall be opened.

9 Or what man is there of you, whom if his son ask bread, will he give him a stone?

第七章

一、你們不要議論人、免得你們被議論、二、你們怎樣議論人、也必怎樣被議論、你們怎麼量人人也怎樣度量你們、三、為甚麼看見你兄弟眼中有刺倒不覺自己眼中有梁木呢、你眼中有梁木怎能對兄弟說容我替你撥出眼中的刺來呢、假冒為善的人、你先將自己眼中的梁木除去、纔能看得清楚、將你兄弟眼中的刺撥出來呢、不可將聖物給狗、不可將你的珍珠丟給豬恐怕踐踏珍珠、轉過來咬你們、你祈求、就必給你們尋找就必尋見叩門、就必給你們開門因為凡祈求的就得著尋找的就尋見叩門的就給他開門。你們中間誰有兒子求餅倒給他石頭呢、

10 Or if he ask a fish, will he give him a serpent?
11 If ye then, being evil, know how to give good gifts unto your children, how much more shall your Father which is in heaven give good things to them that ask him?
12 Therefore all things whatsoever ye would that men should do to you, do ye even so to them: for this is the law and the prophets.
13 ¶ Enter ye in at the strait gate: for wide *is* the gate, and broad *is* the way, that leadeth to destruction, and many there be which go in thereat:
14 Because strait *is* the gate, and narrow *is* the way, which leadeth unto life, and few there be that find it.
15 ¶ Beware of false prophets, which come to you in sheep's clothing, but inwardly they are ravening wolves.
16 Ye shall know them by their fruits. Do men gather grapes of thorns, or figs of thistles?
17 Even so every good tree bringeth forth good fruit; but a corrupt tree bringeth forth evil fruit.
18 A good tree cannot bring forth evil fruit, neither *can* a corrupt tree bring forth good fruit.
19 Every tree that bringeth not forth good fruit is hewn down, and cast into the fire.

求魚倒給他蛇呢。你們雖然不好、尚且知道拏好東西給兒女、何況你們在天上的父、豈不更將好處賜給求他的人麼。你們要人怎樣待你們、你們也當怎樣待人這就是律法和先知書的大旨。○你們要進窄門、因爲領到滅亡地方的門是寬的路是大的、進去的人多、領到永生地方的門是窄的路是小的、找著的人少。○你們謹防假先知那樣人到你們這裏來、外面像羊裏面是豺狼你們看他們所結的果子、就可以認出他們來、荊棘裏豈能摘葡萄呢、蒺藜裏豈能採無花果呢。好樹結好果子、不好樹結不好果子、好樹不能結不好果子、不好樹不能結好果子、凡不結好果子的樹、就砍了丟在火裏。

20 Wherefore by their fruits ye shall know them.

21 ¶ Not every one that saith unto me, Lord, Lord, shall enter into the kingdom of heaven; but he that doeth the will of my Father which is in heaven.

22 Many will say to me in that day, Lord, Lord, have we prophesied in thy name? and in thy name have cast out devils? and in thy name done many wonderful works?

23 And then will I profess unto them, I never knew you: depart from me, ye that work iniquity.

24 ¶ Therefore whosoever heareth these sayings of mine, and doeth them, I will liken him unto a wise man, which built his house upon a rock:

25 And the rain descended, and the floods came, and the winds blew, and beat upon that house; and it fell not: for it was founded upon a rock.

26 And every one that heareth these sayings of mine, and doeth them not, shall be likened unto a foolish man, which built his house upon the sand:

27 And the rain descended, and the floods came, and the winds blew, and beat upon that house; and it fell: and great was the fall of it.

28 And it came to pass, when Jesus had ended these sayings, the people were astonished at his doctrine:

所以你們看他們結的果子、就可以認出他們來了。○凡稱呼我說、主阿、主阿的人、未必都能進天國、惟獨遵行我天父旨意的、纔能進去、當那日子必有許多人對我說、主阿、主阿、我不是奉你的名傳教奉你的名趕鬼泰你的名作許多奇事麼、我就明明告訴他們說、我不曾認得你們、你們這些作惡的人、離開我去罷。凡聽見我這話就去行的、這人如同聰明人、在磐石上蓋造房子、雨淋、水淹、風吹、撞著那房子、房子總不倒塌、因爲根基在磐石上。凡聽見我這話不去行的、這人如同恩拙人、在沙土上蓋造房子、雨淋、水淹、風吹、撞著那房子、房子就倒塌了、並且倒塌得很大。耶穌講完了話、衆人聽他的教訓、都甚詫異

ST. MATTHEW.

29 For he taught them as *one* having authority, and not as the scribes.

CHAPTER 8.

WHEN he was come down from the mountain, great multitudes followed him.

2 And, behold, there came a leper and worshipped him, saying, Lord, if thou wilt, thou canst make me clean.

3 And Jesus put forth *his* hand, and touched him, saying, I will; be thou clean. And immediately his leprosy was cleansed.

4 And Jesus saith unto him, See thou tell no man; but go thy way, shew thyself to the priest, and offer the gift that Moses commanded, for a testimony unto them.

5 ¶ And when Jesus was entered into Capernaum, there came unto him a centurion, beseeching him,

6 And saying, Lord, my servant lieth at home sick of the palsy, grievously tormented.

7 And Jesus saith unto him, I will come and heal him.

8 The centurion answered and said, Lord, I am not worthy that thou shouldest come under my roof: but speak the word only, and my servant shall be healed.

因爲他教訓人、正如有權柄的人、不同那讀書人。

第八章

耶穌下山許多的人跟隨他有一個長癩的人來拜耶穌說、主若肯必能叫我乾淨了、耶穌伸手摸他說、我肯你乾淨了罷他的癩立刻就乾淨了、耶穌對他說、你要謹愼不可告訴人要去叫祭司察看你的身體獻上摩西所吩咐的禮物、在衆人面前做憑據。○耶穌進了迦百農、有一個百夫長進前來求他說、主阿我的僕人患癱瘋病、在屋裏躺臥、甚是疼痛耶穌說我去醫治他、百夫長回答說、主到我家我不敢當、只求說一句話我的僕人就必好了、

ST. MATTHEW.

9 For I am a man under authority, having soldiers under me: and I say to this *man*, Go, and he goeth; and to another, Come, and he cometh; and to my servant, Do this, and he doeth *it*.

10 When Jesus heard *it*, he marvelled, and said to them that followed, Verily I say unto you, I have not found so great faith, no, not in Israel.

11 And I say unto you, That many shall come from the east and west, and shall sit down with Abraham, and Isaac, and Jacob, in the kingdom of heaven:

12 But the children of the kingdom shall be cast out into outer darkness: there shall be weeping and gnashing of teeth.

13 And Jesus said unto the centurion, Go thy way; and as thou hast believed, *so* be it done unto thee. And his servant was healed in the selfsame hour.

14 ¶ And when Jesus was come into Peter's house, he saw his wife's mother laid, and sick of a fever.

15 And he touched her hand, and the fever left her: and she arose, and ministered unto them.

馬太第八章

因為我屬人管、也有兵屬我管、叫這個去就去、叫那個來就來、吩咐我的僕人作這事、他就去作。耶穌聽見就詫異、對跟從的人說、我實在告訴你們、這樣深信的、就是在以色列人中也沒有遇見過。我又告訴你們、從東從西將有許多人來、在天國與亞伯拉罕以撒雅各一同坐席。反將本國的子民趕逐到外邊黑暗地方去、在那裏必要哀哭切齒了。耶穌對百夫長說你回去罷照著你的信與你成全了、他僕人立時就好了。○耶穌到了彼得家裏看見他岳母患熱病躺臥、耶穌一摸他的手熱病退了、他就起來服事他們。

ST. MATTHEW.

16 ¶ When the even was come, they brought unto him many that were possessed with devils: and he cast out the spirits with *his* word, and healed all that were sick:

17 That it might be fulfilled which was spoken by Esaias the prophet, saying, Himself took our infirmities, and bare *our* sicknesses.

18 ¶ Now when Jesus saw great multitudes about him, he gave commandment to depart unto the other side.

19 And a certain scribe came, and said unto him, Master, I will follow thee whithersoever thou goest.

20 And Jesus saith unto him, The foxes have holes, and the birds of the air *have* nests; but the Son of man hath not where to lay *his* head.

21 And another of his disciples said unto him, Lord, suffer me first to go and bury my father.

22 But Jesus said unto him, Follow me; and let the dead bury their dead.

23 ¶ And when he was entered into a ship, his disciples followed him.

24 And, behold, there arose a great tempest in the sea, insomuch that the ship was covered with the waves: but he was asleep.

25 And his disciples came to *him*, and awoke him, saying, Lord, save us: we perish.

到了晚上、有人帶著許多被鬼附的、來到耶穌面前、耶穌只用一句話、將鬼都趕出去了、並且醫好一切有病的人、這正應驗先知以賽亞所說他承攬我們的病患擔當我們的疾痛的話了。○耶穌見許多人圍繞自己就吩咐門徒渡到那邊岸上去。有一個讀書人進前來說夫子、無論往那裏去我要跟從你。耶穌說、狐狸有洞飛鳥有巢惟獨人子沒有安身的地方又有一個門徒對耶穌說、主阿容我先回去葬我父親、耶穌說讓死人葬埋他們的死人去、你跟從我罷。○耶穌上了船、門徒跟從他海裏忽然起了暴風波浪幾乎掩蓋了船那時候耶穌正睡覺門徒來叫醒他說、主救我們我們要死了。

ST. MATTHEW.

26 And he saith unto them, Why are ye fearful, O ye of little faith? Then he arose, and rebuked the winds and the sea; and there was a great calm.

27 But the men marvelled, saying, What manner of man is this, that even the winds and the sea obey him!

28 ¶ And when he was come to the other side into the country of the Gergesenes, there met him two possessed with devils, coming out of the tombs, exceeding fierce, so that no man might pass by that way.

29 And, behold, they cried out, saying, What have we to do with thee, Jesus, thou Son of God? art thou come hither to torment us before the time?

30 And there was a good way off from them a herd of many swine feeding.

31 So the devils besought him, saying, If thou cast us out, suffer us to go away into the herd of swine.

32 And he said unto them, Go. And when they were come out, they went into the herd of swine: and, behold, the whole herd of swine ran violently down a steep place into the sea, and perished in the waters.

33 And they that kept them fled, and went their ways into the city, and told every thing, and what was befallen to the possessed of the devils.

馬太第八章

耶穌說、你們這小信的人、為甚麼懼怕、於是起來指斥風浪、海就大大平靜了。眾人都詫異說他是怎樣的人、風和海也聽從他。○耶穌渡過海、到了革革沙地方、遇見兩個被鬼附的人、從墳墓裏出來、甚是兇猛、向來沒有人敢從那條路上經過他們呼叫說、神的兒子耶穌、我們與你有甚麼相干、時候沒有到、你就來了叫我們受苦麼、遠遠的有一羣豬在那裏喫食、鬼求耶穌說若要趕出我們、容我進豬羣裏附著豬去、耶穌說去罷鬼就出離人身、進入豬羣、那羣豬忽然闖下山坡、投在海裏淹死了。放豬的人跑進城去、將這事和被鬼附的人的情節、都告訴城裏的人。

ST. MATTHEW.

34 And, behold, the whole city came out to meet Jesus: and when they saw him, they besought *him* that he would depart out of their coasts.

CHAPTER 9.

AND he entered into a ship, and passed over, and came into his own city.

2 And, behold, they brought to him a man sick of the palsy, lying on a bed: and Jesus seeing their faith said unto the sick of the palsy; Son, be of good cheer; thy sins be forgiven thee.

3 And, behold, certain of the scribes said within themselves, This *man* blasphemeth.

4 And Jesus knowing their thoughts said, Wherefore think ye evil in your hearts?

5 For whether is easier, to say, *Thy* sins be forgiven thee; or to say, Arise, and walk?

6 But that ye may know that the Son of man hath power on earth to forgive sins, (then saith he to the sick of the palsy,) Arise, take up thy bed, and go unto thine house.

7 And he arose, and departed to his house.

8 But when the multitudes saw *it*, they marvelled, and glorified God, which had given such power unto men.

合城的人、都出來見耶穌、求他離開他們的境界。

第九章

耶穌上了船渡過海回到自己城裏、有人擡著一個患癱瘋病躺臥在牀的人、來見耶穌。耶穌見他們這樣信他、就對癱瘋的人說、小子放心你的罪赦了。有幾個讀書人心裏說這人說僭妄的話了。耶穌知道他們的心意就說你們爲甚麼心裏懷著惡念呢、你想或說你的罪赦免、或說你起來行走、那一樣容易。現在要叫你們知道人子在世上有赦罪的權柄、就對癱瘋的人說、起來、拏你的牀回家去罷、那人就起來、回家去了。衆人看見詫異、就歸榮耀給神、因爲神將這樣的權柄賜給人。

9 ¶ And as Jesus passed forth from thence, he saw a man, named Matthew sitting at the receipt of custom: and he saith unto him, Follow me. And he arose, and followed him.

10 ¶ And it came to pass, as Jesus sat at meat in the house, behold, many publicans and sinners came and sat down with him and his disciples.

11 And when the Pharisees saw *it*, they said unto his disciples, Why eateth your master with publicans and sinners?

12 But when Jesus heard *that*, he said unto them, They that be whole need not a physician, but they that are sick.

13 But go ye and learn what *that* meaneth, I will have mercy, and not sacrifice: for I am not come to call the righteous, but sinners to repentance.

14 ¶ Then came to him the disciples of John, saying, Why do we and the Pharisees fast oft, but thy disciples fast not?

15 And Jesus said unto them, Can the children of the bridechamber mourn, as long as the bridegroom is with them? but the days will come, when the bridegroom shall be taken from them, and then shall they fast

○耶穌從這裏往前行、看見一個人名叫馬太坐在稅關上、就對他說、你跟從我來、他就起來、跟從了耶穌。耶穌在他家裏坐席、有許多稅吏和罪人來、與耶穌並耶穌的門徒一同坐席。法利賽人看見就問門徒說、你們先生爲甚麼與稅吏並罪人一同喫飯呢。耶穌聽見、就說健壯的人用不著醫生患病的人纔用得著、我喜歡憐恤的事、不歡喜祭祀這句經的意思你們且去揣摩、我來不是要叫人悔改、正是要叫罪人悔改。○那時約翰的門徒來見耶穌、問他說、我們和法利賽人常常禁食你的門徒爲甚麼倒不禁食。耶穌囘答說、新郎和慶賀新郎的人同在的時候、慶賀的人豈能哀慟呢、將來新郎離開他們去了、那時候必要禁食。

16 No man putteth a piece of new cloth unto an old garment; for that which is put in to fill it up taketh from the garment, and the rent is made worse.

17 Neither do men put new wine into old bottles: else the bottles break, and the wine runneth out, and the bottles perish: but they put new wine into new bottles, and both are preserved.

18 ¶ While he spake these things unto them, behold, there came a certain ruler, and worshipped him, saying, My daughter is even now dead: but come and lay thy hand upon her, and she shall live.

19 And Jesus arose, and followed him, and *so did* his disciples.

20 ¶ And, behold, a woman, which was diseased with an issue of blood twelve years, came behind *him*, and touched the hem of his garment:

21 For she said within herself, If I may but touch his garment, I shall be whole.

22 But Jesus turned him about, and when he saw her, he said, Daughter, be of good comfort; thy faith hath made thee whole. And the woman was made whole from that hour.

23 And when Jesus came into the ruler's house and saw the minstrels and the people making a noise,

沒有拏新布補舊衣服的、恐怕所補的新布、反帶壞了舊衣服、破綻更大了。沒有將新酒盛在舊皮袋裏的、恐怕皮袋裂開酒漏出來、連皮袋也壞了、惟將新酒盛在新皮袋裏、兩樣就都保全了。○耶穌正說這話的時候、有一個官來拜他、說我女兒方纔死了、但願你去按手在他身上、他就必活了。耶穌起來、跟隨他去、有一個婦人患了十二年血漏的病、來到耶穌背後、摸他的衣裳穗子、因爲他心裏說、我但摸耶穌的衣裳、就必痊愈、耶穌囘頭看見那婦人、就說女子放心、你的信救了你、從那時候婦人就痊愈了。耶穌到了那官的家裏、看見有吹手又有許多人喧譁、

24 He said unto them, Give place: for the maid is not dead, but sleepeth. And they laughed him to scorn.

25 But when the people were put forth, he went in, and took her by the hand, and the maid arose.

26 And the fame hereof went abroad into all that land.

27 ¶ And when Jesus departed thence, two blind men followed him, crying, and saying, *Thou* Son of David, have mercy on us.

28 And when he was come into the house, the blind men came to him: and Jesus saith unto them, Believe ye that I am able to do this? They said unto him, Yea, Lord.

29 Then touched he their eyes, saying, According to your faith be it unto you.

30 And their eyes were opened; and Jesus straitly charged them, saying, See *that* no man know *it*.

31 But they, when they were departed, spread abroad his fame in all that country.

32 ¶ As they went out, behold, they brought to him a dumb man possessed with a devil.

33 And when the devil was cast out, the dumb spake: and the multitudes marvelled, saying, It was never so seen in Israel.

就對他們說、你們且退去這女孩兒不是死了是睡覺呢、他們都笑他。逐出耶穌就進去拉著女孩兒的手女孩兒就起來了。於是耶穌傳遍了那地方。耶穌從那裏往前走、有兩個瞎子跟在後面、呼叫說大衛的子孫憐恤我們。耶穌進了房子、瞎子就來到他面前、耶穌對他們說你們信我能做這事不信、瞎子說、主、我們信。耶穌就摸他們的眼睛說、照著你們的信與你們成全了罷。他們的眼睛就能看見了。耶穌切切的囑咐他們說、你們要小心不可叫人知道。他們出去後、有人領著一個啞吧、是被鬼附的、來到耶穌的面前、耶穌將鬼趕出去、啞吧就說話了、衆人都以為希奇說、在以色列人中間從來沒有看見這樣的事。

ST. MATTHEW.

34 But the Pharisees said, He casteth out devils through the prince of the devils.

35 And Jesus went about all the cities and villages, teaching in their synagogues, and preaching the gospel of the kingdom, and healing every sickness and every disease among the people.

36 ¶ But when he saw the multitudes, he was moved with compassion on them, because they fainted, and were scattered abroad, as sheep having no shepherd.

37 Then saith he unto his disciples, The harvest truly *is* plenteous, but the labourers *are* few;

38 Pray ye therefore the Lord of the harvest, that he will send forth labourers into his harvest.

CHAPTER 10.

AND when he had called unto *him* his twelve disciples, he gave them power *against* unclean spirits, to cast them out, and to heal all manner of sickness and all manner of disease.

2 Now the names of the twelve apostles are these; The first, Simon, who is called Peter, and Andrew his brother; James *the son* of Zebedee, and John his brother;

馬太第十章　33

法利賽人說、他是靠著鬼王趕鬼的。○耶穌走遍各城各鄉、在會堂裏教訓人、宣講天國的福音、醫治民間各樣的病患疾痛、看見大衆的人、就憐恤他們、因爲他們困苦流離、如同羊沒有牧養的人一般、耶穌對門徒說要收的莊稼多、作工的人少、當求莊稼的主、多遣工人、去收他的莊稼。

第十章

耶穌叫了十二個門徒來、賜給他們權柄、叫他們能逐出邪鬼、醫好各樣疾病。這十二使徒的名、頭一個叫西門、又稱彼得、還有他兄弟安得烈、西庇太的兒子雅各和雅各的兄弟約翰、

34 ST. MATTHEW.

3 Philip, and Bartholomew; Thomas, and Matthew the publican; James *the son of* Alpheus, and Lebbeus, whose surname was Thaddeus;

4 Simon the Canaanite, and Judas Iscariot, who also betrayed him.

5 These twelve Jesus sent forth, and commanded them, saying, Go not into the way of the Gentiles, and into *any* city of the Samaritans enter ye not:

6 But go rather to the lost sheep of the house of Israel.

7 And as ye go, preach, saying, The kingdom of heaven is at hand.

8 Heal the sick, cleanse the lepers, raise the dead, cast out devils: freely ye have received, freely give.

9 Provide neither gold, nor silver, nor brass in your purses;

10 Nor scrip for *your* journey, neither two coats, neither shoes, nor yet staves: for the workman is worthy of his meat.

11 And into whatsoever city or town ye shall enter, inquire who in it is worthy; and there abide till ye go thence.

12 And when ye come into a house, salute it.

13 And if the house be worthy, let your peace come upon it: but if it be not worthy, let your peace return to you.

馬太第十章

腓力、巴多羅買、多瑪、稅吏馬太、亞勒腓的兒子雅各、勒拜又稱達太、西門又稱銳邊、

有賣耶穌的以色加略猶大。○耶穌差遣這十二使徒的時候吩咐他們說外邦人的道路你們不要走撒馬利亞人的城邑你們不要進去。

寧可往以色列家迷失的羊那裏去。你們到處宣傳說天國近了。有病的醫好他長癩的治乾淨他叫死人復活將邪鬼趕出你們白白的得來、也當白白的捨去你們腰袋裏不要帶金銀和銅錢、行

路不要帶口袋、不要帶兩套衣服、也不要帶鞋和拐杖因爲工人得飲食是應當的。

你們無論到了那城那鄉要訪問那裏誰是好人、就住在他家直住到走的時候進的

人的家去就爲那家的人求平安這一家若當得平安你們所求的平安就必臨到

這家若不當得平安你們所求的平安就歸你們了。

ST. MATTHEW.

14 And whosoever shall not receive you, nor hear your words, when ye depart out of that house or city, shake off the dust of your feet.

15 Verily I say unto you, It shall be more tolerable for the land of Sodom and Gomorrah in the day of judgment, than for that city.

16 ¶ Behold, I send you forth as sheep in the midst of wolves: be ye therefore wise as serpents, and harmless as doves.

17 But beware of men: for they will deliver you up to the councils, and they will scourge you in their synagogues;

18 And ye shall be brought before governors and kings for my sake, for a testimony against them and the Gentiles.

19 But when they deliver you up, take no thought how or what ye shall speak: for it shall be given you in that same hour what ye shall speak.

20 For it is not ye that speak, but the Spirit of your Father which speaketh in you.

21 And the brother shall deliver up the brother to death, and the father the child: and the children shall rise up against *their* parents, and cause them to be put to death.

22 And ye shall be hated of all *men* for my name's sake: but he that endureth to the end shall be saved.

馬太第十章

人若不接待你們、不聽你們的話、你們就離開那家和那城、離開的時候、將脚上的塵土抖下去、我實在告訴你們、到了審判的日子、所多馬蛾摩拉的刑罰、比那地方的刑罰還容易受呢。○我差遣你們去、如同羊入了狼羣、所以你們應當靈巧像蛇、馴良像鴿子、你們要謹防世人、因爲他們必要解你們到公會去、在會堂裏鞭打你們、你們將要爲我的緣故、被解到君王侯伯那裏、對他們和外邦人作見證、解你們的時候、不要憂慮怎樣說話、到那時候、必賜你們當說的話、因爲不是你們自己說、是你們的父、聖靈在你們裏面說的。那時候弟兄要將弟兄父親要將兒子送到死地兒女要與父母爲仇害死他們、你們必要爲我的名被衆人怨恨能忍耐到底的必定得救。

23 But when they persecute you in this city, flee ye into another: for verily I say unto you, Ye shall not have gone over the cities of Israel, till the Son of man be come.

24 The disciple is not above *his* master, nor the servant above his lord.

25 It is enough for the disciple that he be as his master, and the servant as his lord. If they have called the master of the house Beelzebub, how much more *shall they call* them of his household?

26 Fear them not therefore: for there is nothing covered, that shall not be revealed; and hid, that shall not be known.

27 What I tell you in darkness, *that* speak ye in light: and what ye hear in the ear, *that* preach ye upon the housetops.

28 And fear not them which kill the body, but are not able to kill the soul: but rather fear him which is able to destroy both soul and body in hell.

29 Are not two sparrows sold for a farthing? and one of them shall not fall on the ground without your Father.

30 But the very hairs of your head are all numbered.

31 Fear ye not therefore, ye are of more value than many sparrows.

有人在這城裏追趕你們、就逃到那城裏去、我實在告訴你們、以色列的城邑你們沒有走遍人子就到了。學生不能越過先生、僕人不能越過家主、學生和先生一樣、僕人和家主一樣也就罷了。人既罵家主是別西卜何況他的家人呢。你們不要懼怕他們、因爲沒有掩藏的事、不露出來的、沒有隱瞞的事、不被人知道的。我在暗中告訴你們的、你們要在明處說出來、我附耳說給你們聽的話、要在房上宣揚出來。那能殺身體、不能殺靈魂的、不要怕他、能將身體和靈魂、都滅在地獄裏的、正要怕他。兩個雀鳥、不是一分銀子買的麽、若不是天父的意思、一個也不能掉在地上的。你們的頭髮、也都被數過了。所以不要懼怕、你們比許多的雀鳥貴重多了。

ST. MATTHEW.

32 Whosoever therefore shall confess me before men, him will I confess also before my Father which is in heaven.

33 But whosoever shall deny me before men, him will I also deny before my Father which is in heaven.

34 Think not that I am come to send peace on earth: I came not to send peace, but a sword.

35 For I am come to set a man at variance against his father, and the daughter against her mother, and the daughter in law against her mother in law.

36 And a man's foes *shall be* they of his own household.

37 He that loveth father or mother more than me is not worthy of me: and he that loveth son or daughter more than me is not worthy of me.

38 And he that taketh not his cross, and followeth after me, is not worthy of me.

39 He that findeth his life shall lose it: and he that loseth his life for my sake shall find it.

40 ¶ He that receiveth you receiveth me; and he that receiveth me receiveth him that sent me.

41 He that receiveth a prophet in the name of a prophet shall receive a prophet's reward; and he that receiveth a righteous man in the name of a righteous man shall receive a righteous man's reward.

馬太第十章

凡在人面前認我的、我在我天父面前也認他。在人面前不認我的、我在我天父面前也不認他。你們不要想我來、是叫世界上太平、我來並不是叫世界上太平、乃是叫世界上動刀兵。我來了、兒子要和父親生疏、女兒要和母親生疏、媳婦要和婆婆生疏、人的仇敵、就是自己家裏的人。愛父母勝似愛我的、不配作我的門徒、愛子女勝似愛我的、不配作我的門徒。不背著十字架跟從我的、也不配作我的門徒。得著生命的、必要失喪生命、爲我失喪生命的、必要得著生命。接待你們、就是接待我、接待我、就是接待差我來的父。有人接待先知、因爲他是先知、就必得先知所得的賞賜。

38 ST. MATTHEW.

42 And whosoever shall give to drink unto one of these little ones a cup of cold *water* only in the name of a disciple, verily I say unto you, he shall in no wise lose his reward.

CHAPTER II.

AND it came to pass, when Jesus had made an end of commanding his twelve disciples, he departed thence to teach and to preach in their cities.

2 Now when John had heard in the prison the works of Christ, he sent two of his disciples,

3 And said unto him, Art thou he that should come, or do we look for another?

4 Jesus answered and said unto them, Go and shew John again those things which ye do hear and see:

5 The blind receive their sight, and the lame walk, the lepers are cleansed, and the deaf hear, the dead are raised up, and the poor have the gospel preached to them.

6 And blessed is *he*, whosoever shall not be offended in me.

7 ¶ And as they departed, Jesus began to say unto the multitudes concerning John, What went ye out into the wilderness to see? A reed shaken with the wind?

馬太第十一章

第十一章

一耶穌吩附完了十二個門徒、就離開那裏、往各城裏教訓人、傳道去了。二那時候約翰在監裏聽見基督所作的事、就差遣兩個門徒去、問耶穌說應當來的是你呢還是我們等候別人呢。四耶穌回答說、你們將所看見所聽見的、去告訴約翰、就是瞎眼的看見、瘸腿的行走、長癩的乾淨、耳聾的聽見、死了的復活、貧窮的得聽福音。凡不厭棄我的就有福了。○約翰的門徒去後耶穌對衆人講論約翰說、你們從前到曠野裏去、是要看甚麼、要看風吹動的蘆葦麼。

有人接待義人、因爲他是義人、就必得義人所得的賞賜。有人但將一杯冷水給這小子裏的一個人喝、因爲他是門徒、我實在告訴你們、這人沒有不得賞賜的了。

ST. MATTHEW.

8 But what went ye out for to see? A man clothed in soft raiment? behold, they that wear soft *clothing* are in kings' houses.

9 But what went ye out for to see? A prophet? yea, I say unto you, and more than a prophet.

10 For this is he, of whom it is written, Behold, I send my messenger before thy face, which shall prepare thy way before thee.

11 Verily I say unto you, Among them that are born of women there hath not risen a greater than John the Baptist: notwithstanding, he that is least in the kingdom of heaven is greater than he.

12 And from the days of John the Baptist until now the kingdom of heaven suffereth violence, and the violent take it by force.

13 For all the prophets and the law prophesied until John.

14 And if ye will receive *it*, this is Elias, which was for to come.

15 He that hath ears to hear, let him hear.

16 ¶ But whereunto shall I liken this generation? It is like unto children sitting in the markets, and calling unto their fellows,

17 And saying, We have piped unto you, and ye have not danced; we have mourned unto you, and ye have not lamented.

馬太第十一章

你們出去是要看甚麼、要看穿華美衣服的人麼、穿華美衣服的人、是在王宮裏的。

你們出去究竟是要看甚麼、要看先知麼、我實在告訴你們、這人比先知更大。

經上說、我差遣我的使者在你前頭預備你的道路、這話就是指著這人說的。

我實在告訴你們、凡婦人所生的、沒有大過施洗約翰的、然而天國裏最小的人、還比他大。

從施洗約翰的時候到如今、人人努力要得天國、努力的人就得著了。

眾先知和律法書、說未來的事、到約翰為止。○

我對你們說、你們若肯聽我就告訴你們、這人就是應當來的以利亞、有耳可聽的、都應當聽。

我拏甚麼比現今的世代、就如孩童坐在街上、招呼他們的同伴、說、我對你們吹笛、你們不舞跳、我對你們舉哀、你們不號哭。

18 For John came neither eating nor drinking, and they say, He hath a devil.

19 The Son of man came eating and drinking, and they say, Behold a man gluttonous, and a wine-bibber, a friend of publicans and sinners. But wisdom is justified of her children.

20 ¶ Then began he to upbraid the cities wherein most of his mighty works were done, because they repented not:

21 Woe unto thee, Chorazin! woe unto thee, Bethsaida! for if the mighty works, which were done in you, had been done in Tyre and Sidon, they would have repented long ago in sackcloth and ashes.

22 But I say unto you, It shall be more tolerable for Tyre and Sidon at the day of judgment, than for you.

23 And thou, Capernaum, which art exalted unto heaven, shalt be brought down to hell: for if the mighty works, which have been done in thee, had been done in Sodom, it would have remained until this day.

24 But I say unto you, That it shall be more tolerable for the land of Sodom in the day of judgment, than for thee.

約翰來了、不喫不喝、人就說他是被鬼附的、人子來了、也喫也喝、人又說他是貪食好酒的人、是稅吏罪人的朋友、但有道的人總以道爲是。○耶穌在各城裏施暴能許多的異能、他們仍是不悔改、就在那時候責備他們、說哥拉汛是有禍的伯賽大也是有禍的、我在你們中間所作的奇事、若作在推羅西頓、那裏的人早已披蔴蒙灰悔改了。我告訴你們、當審判的日子推羅西頓的刑罰比你們的刑罰還容易忍受。迦百農、你已經升到天上、後來必要墮落在地獄裏、因爲在你耶所作的奇事、若作在所多馬、那地方還可以存到今日。我告訴你們、當審判的日子所多馬的刑罰比你們的刑罰還容易忍受。

ST. MATTHEW.

¶ At that time Jesus
─red and said, I thank
O Father, Lord of heaven
─arth, because thou hast
─ese things from the wise
─rudent, and hast revealed
unto babes.

Even so, Father; for so
─ned good in thy sight.

All things are delivered
─ne of my Father: and no
─noweth the Son, but the
─r; neither knoweth any
─he Father, save the Son,
─e to whomsoever the Son
─veal *him*.

¶ Come unto me, all *ye*
─labour and are heavy
─ and I will give you rest.

Take my yoke upon you,
─arn of me; for I am meek
─owly in heart: and ye
─ind rest unto your souls.

For my yoke *is* easy, and
─rden is light.

CHAPTER 12.

─ that time Jesus went on
─ the sabbath day through
─orn; and his disciples
─ hungered, and began to
─ the ears of corn, and

─it when the Pharisees
─, they said unto him,
─l, thy disciples do that
─is not lawful to do upon
─bath day.

馬太第十二章　41

○那時、耶穌說父天地的、主我讚美你、因為你將這道理、對著聰明通達人就藏起來、對著嬰孩就顯出來父阿、是這樣的、因為你的意旨本是如此的、萬物都是我父交付我的、除了父沒有人知道子、除了子和子所願意指教的沒有人知道父、○凡勞苦背負重擔的人可到我這裏來、我要賜給你們平安、我心裏柔和謙遜、你們應當負我的軛學我的樣式這樣你們心裏必得平安、因為我叫你們負的軛是容易的叫你們挑的擔是輕省的。

第十二章

那時、耶穌在安息日、從麥田經過門徒餓了、就摘麥穗喫。法利賽人看見就對耶穌說你的門徒作安息日不當作的事了。

3 But he said unto them, Have ye not read what David did, when he was a hungered, and they that were with him;

4 How he entered into the house of God, and did eat the shewbread, which was not lawful for him to eat, neither for them which were with him, but only for the priests?

5 Or have ye not read in the law, how that on the sabbath days the priests in the temple profane the sabbath, and are blameless?

6 But I say unto you, That in this place is *one* greater than the temple.

7 But if ye had known what *this* meaneth, I will have mercy, and not sacrifice, ye would not have condemned the guiltless.

8 For the Son of man is Lord even of the sabbath day.

9 And when he was departed thence, he went into their synagogue:

10 ¶ And, behold, there was a man which had *his* hand withered. And they asked him, saying, Is it lawful to heal on the sabbath days? that they might accuse him.

11 And he said unto them, What man shall there be among you, that shall have one sheep, and if it fall into a pit on the sabbath day, will he not lay hold on it, and lift *it* out?

St. MATTHEW.

12 How much then is a man better than a sheep? Wherefore it is lawful to do well on the sabbath days.

13 Then saith he to the man, Stretch forth thine hand. And he stretched it forth; and it was restored whole, like as the other.

14 ¶ Then the Pharisees went out, and held a council against him, how they might destroy him.

15 But when Jesus knew it, he withdrew himself from thence: and great multitudes followed him, and he healed them all;

16 And charged them that they should not make him known:

17 That it might be fulfilled which was spoken by Esaias the prophet, saying,

18 Behold my servant, whom I have chosen; my beloved, in whom my soul is well pleased: I will put my Spirit upon him, and he shall shew judgment to the Gentiles.

19 He shall not strive, nor cry; neither shall any man hear his voice in the streets.

20 A bruised reed shall he not break, and smoking flax shall he not quench, till he send forth judgment unto victory.

21 And in his name shall the Gentiles trust.

十二人不比羊貴重得多麼、所以安息日作善事、是可以的、就對那人說、伸出手來。他將手一伸、手就好了、和那隻手一樣。○法利賽人出去、商議怎樣可以殺害耶穌。十五耶穌知道了、就離開那裏、有許多人跟從他、耶穌將他們中間的病人、都醫好了、囑咐他們、不要將他宣揚出來。這就應了先知以賽亞的話、說我所揀選所疼愛心裏所喜悅的僕人、我要將我的聖靈賜給他他必將眞道指敎列邦人他不爭競、不喧嚷、街市上沒有人聽見他的聲音受傷的蘆葦他不折斷將殘的燈火他不吹滅並且施行眞道叫眞道得勝異邦人也仰望他的名了。

22 ¶ Then was brought unto him one possessed with a devil, blind, and dumb: and he healed him, insomuch that the blind and dumb both spake and saw.

23 And all the people were amazed, and said, Is not this the Son of David?

24 But when the Pharisees heard *it*, they said, This *fellow* doth not cast out devils, but by Beelzebub the prince of the devils.

25 And Jesus knew their thoughts, and said unto them, Every kingdom divided against itself is brought to desolation; and every city or house divided against itself shall not stand:

26 And if Satan cast out Satan, he is divided against himself; how shall then his kingdom stand?

27 And if I by Beelzebub cast out devils, by whom do your children cast *them* out? therefore they shall be your judges.

28 But if I cast out devils by the Spirit of God, then the kingdom of God is come unto you.

29 Or else, how can one enter into a strong man's house, and spoil his goods, except he first bind the strong man? and then he will spoil his house.

30 He that is not with me is against me; and he that gathereth not with me scattereth abroad.

○那時候、有人帶著一個被鬼附著又瞎又啞的人、到耶穌面前、耶穌醫治他、叫他瞎眼能看見啞吧能說話。眾人都詫異說這不是大衛的子孫麽。法利賽人聽見就說他趕鬼無非是靠著鬼王別西卜阿耶穌知道他們的意念就對他們說凡一國自相分爭必要滅亡一城一家自相分爭必站立不住。若撒但趕撒但、就是自相分爭他的國如何立得住呢若我靠著別西卜趕鬼、你們的子弟趕鬼又靠著誰呢、這樣他們就必說你們是有錯的。若我靠著真神的聖靈趕鬼、神的國就臨到你們這裏了人如何能進勇士家裏、搶掠他的傢具呢不是先捆住勇士、後纔可以搶掠他的家財麽。不與我同心就是攻打我的、不同我收斂就是分散的。

St. MATTHEW.

31 ¶ Wherefore I say unto you, All manner of sin and blasphemy shall be forgiven unto men: but the blasphemy *against* the *Holy* Ghost shall not be forgiven unto men.

32 And whosoever speaketh a word against the Son of man, it shall be forgiven him: but whosoever speaketh against the Holy Ghost, it shall not be forgiven him, neither in this world, neither in the *world* to come.

33 Either make the tree good, and his fruit good; or else make the tree corrupt, and his fruit corrupt: for the tree is known by *his* fruit.

34 O generation of vipers, how can ye, being evil, speak good things? for out of the abundance of the heart the mouth speaketh.

35 A good man out of the good treasure of the heart bringeth forth good things: and an evil man out of the evil treasure bringeth forth evil things.

36 But I say unto you, That every idle word that men shall speak, they shall give account thereof in the day of judgment.

37 For by thy words thou shalt be justified, and by thy words thou shalt be condemned.

38 ¶ Then certain of the scribes and of the Pharisees answered, saying, Master, we would see a sign from thee.

馬太第十二章

³¹所以我告訴你們、人無論犯甚麼罪、無論毀謗誰、都可以蒙赦免、若毀謗聖靈的、今世來世永不赦免他。凡毀謗人子的、還可赦免他、毀謗聖靈的、今世來世永不赦免他。³³你們旣是惡人、怎能說出好話來呢、因爲心裏存著甚麼、嘴裏就說甚麼。善人心裏存著善、就發出善來、惡人心裏存著惡、就發出惡來。³⁶我告訴你們、凡人所說的虛妄的話、到審判的日子、必要句句究問他。³⁷因爲憑你的話定你爲義人、也憑你的話定你爲罪人。○³⁸當時有幾個讀書人和法利賽人對耶穌說、請夫子作奇蹟給我們看。

39 But he answered and said unto them, An evil and adulterous generation seeketh after a sign; and there shall no sign be given to it, but the sign of the prophet Jonas:

40 For as Jonas was three days and three nights in the whale's belly; so shall the Son of man be three days and three nights in the heart of the earth.

41 The men of Nineveh shall rise in judgment with this generation, and shall condemn it: because they repented at the preaching of Jonas; and, behold, a greater than Jonas is here.

42 The queen of the south shall rise up in the judgment with this generation, and shall condemn it: for she came from the uttermost parts of the earth to hear the wisdom of Solomon; and behold, a greater than Solomon is here.

43 When the unclean spirit is gone out of a man, he walketh through dry places, seeking rest, and findeth none.

44 Then he saith, I will return into my house from whence I came out; and when he is come, he findeth it empty, swept, and garnished.

³⁹耶穌回答說、奸惡的世代要看奇蹟、除了先知約拏的奇蹟之外、沒有甚麼奇蹟與你們看。約拏⁴⁰三日三夜在大魚腹中、人子也要三日三夜在地裏頭。尼尼微的人當審判的日子要起來定這世代的罪、因爲他們聽了約拏的勸化、就悔改了、在這裏還有比約拏更大的呢。南方的女王當審判的日子要起來定這世代的罪、因爲他從地邊上來要聽所羅門智慧的話、在這裏還有比所羅門更大的呢。⁴³邪鬼離了人、就在無水的野地走來走去尋找安息的地方、竟尋不著。於是說不如回到我所出來的屋子去。到了那裏看見裏面空閒、打掃乾淨、修飾好了。

ST. MATTHEW.

45 Then goeth he, and taketh with himself seven other spirits more wicked than himself, and they enter in and dwell there: and the last *state* of that man is worse than the first. Even so shall it be also unto this wicked generation.

46 ¶ While he yet talked to the people, behold, *his* mother and his brethren stood without, desiring to speak with him.

47 Then one said unto him, Behold, thy mother and thy brethren stand without, desiring to speak with thee.

48 But he answered and said unto him that told him, Who is my mother? and who are my brethren?

49 And he stretched forth his hand toward his disciples, and said, Behold my mother and my brethren!

50 For whosoever shall do the will of my Father which is in heaven, the same is my brother, and sister, and mother.

CHAPTER 13.

THE same day went Jesus out of the house, and sat by the sea side.

2 And great multitudes were gathered together unto him, so that he went into a ship, and sat; and the whole multitude stood on the shore.

3 And he spake many things unto them in parables, saying, Behold, a sower went forth to sow;

馬太第十三章

就去帶了七個比自己還兇惡的鬼進去住著、那個人的後患比從前更甚了。這奸惡的世代、也必要如此。○耶穌同眾人說話的時候他母親和他弟兄站在外邊要同他說話、有人告訴耶穌說、你母親和你弟兄站在外邊要同你說話、耶穌回答說、誰是我的母親誰是我的弟兄。就伸手指著門徒說你們看我的母親、我的弟兄。凡遵我天父旨意行的人就是我的弟兄姐妹和母親了。

第十三章

當日耶穌從房子裏出來、坐在海邊。二有許多人聚集在他面前、耶穌就上船坐下、眾人都站在岸上耶穌用許多比喻對他們講道、說有撒種的人出去撒種。

48 ST. MATTHEW.

4 And when he sowed, some *seeds* fell by the wayside, and the fowls came and devoured them up:

5 Some fell upon stony places, where they had not much earth: and forthwith they sprung up, because they had no deepness of earth:

6 And when the sun was up, they were scorched; and because they had no root, they withered away.

7 And some fell among thorns; and the thorns sprung up, and choked them:

8 But other fell into good ground, and brought forth fruit, some a hundredfold, some sixtyfold, some thirtyfold.

9 Who hath ears to hear, let him hear.

10 And the disciples came, and said unto him, Why speakest thou unto them in parables?

11 He answered and said unto them, Because it is given unto you to know the mysteries of the kingdom of heaven, but to them it is not given.

12 For whosoever hath, to him shall be given, and he shall have more abundance: but whosoever hath not, from him shall be taken away even that he hath.

13 Therefore speak I to them in parables; because they seeing see not; and hearing they hear not, neither do they understand.

馬太第十三章

撒的時候、有落在道旁的、雀鳥來喫盡了。有落在土薄有石頭的地上、土既淺薄、發苗最快、日頭出來一曬、因為沒有根就枯乾了。有落在荊棘裏的、荊棘長起來、將苗遮蔽住了。有落在好土裏的、結實有一百倍的、有六十倍的、有三十倍的。凡有耳可聽的都應當聽。門徒進前來問耶穌說對眾人講話為甚麼用比喻耶穌回答說、因為天國的奧秘只賜與你們知道、不賜與他們知道。凡有的還要加給他、叫他有餘、沒有的、連他所有的、也要奪過來、我向他們說比喻的話、因為他們是看也看不見、聽也聽不見、總不省悟。

ST. MATTHEW.

14 And in them is fulfilled the prophecy of Esaias, which saith, By hearing ye shall hear, and shall not understand; and seeing ye shall see, and shall not perceive:

15 For this people's heart is waxed gross, and *their* ears are dull of hearing, and their eyes they have closed; lest at any time they should see with *their* eyes, and hear with *their* ears, and should understand with *their* heart, and should be converted, and I should heal them.

16 But blessed *are* your eyes, for they see: and your ears, for they hear.

17 For verily I say unto you, That many prophets and righteous *men* have desired to see *those things* which ye see, and have not seen *them;* and to hear *those things* which ye hear, and have not heard *them.*

18 ¶ Hear ye therefore the parable of the sower.

19 When any one heareth the word of the kingdom, and understandeth *it* not, then cometh the wicked one, and catcheth away that which was sown in his heart. This is he which received seed by the way side.

20 But he that received the seed into stony places, the same is he that heareth the word, and anon with joy receiveth it;

十四 這些人正應了以賽亞的預言說、你們將來聽見也不省悟、看見也不曉得、因爲這百姓心裏愚頑掩耳不聽閉眼不看、恐怕眼睛看見、耳朵聽見、心裏省悟改了、我就醫治他。十六 你們的眼睛是有福的因爲看見了、你們的耳朵是有福的因爲聽見了。十七 我實在告訴你們、從前有許多先知和義人、要看你們所看的不得看見、要聽你們所聽的不得聽見所以撒種的比喻你們應當聽。十九 凡聽見天國的道理不明白那兇惡的來、將所撒在他心裏的奪了去這就是撒在道旁的了。二十 撒在有石頭的地上的、就是人聽道當下歡喜聽受。

21 Yet hath he not root in himself, but dureth for a while; for when tribulation or persecution ariseth because of the word, by and by he is offended.

22 He also that received seed among the thorns is he that heareth the word; and the care of this world, and the deceitfulness of riches, choke the word, and he becometh unfruitful.

23 But he that received seed into the good ground is he that beareth the word, and understandeth *it*; which also beareth fruit, and bringeth forth, some a hundredfold, some sixty, some thirty.

24 ¶ Another parable put he forth unto them, saying, The kingdom of heaven is likened unto a man which sowed good seed in his field:

25 But while men slept, his enemy came and sowed tares among the wheat, and went his way.

26 But when the blade was sprung up, and brought forth fruit, then appeared the tares also.

27 So the servants of the householder came and said unto him Sir, didst not thou sow good seed in thy field? from whence then hath it tares?

28 He said unto them, An enemy hath done this. The servants said unto him, Wilt thou then that we go and gather them up?

只因他心裏沒有根也不過是暫時的、及至為道遇患難受迫害、就厭棄了撒在荊棘裏的就是人聽道後來世上的思慮貨財的迷惑蔽了道不能結實撒在好地上的就是人聽道明白了後來結實有一百倍的有六十倍的有三十倍的○耶穌又設一個比喻對眾人說天國如同人撒好種在田裏人睡覺的時候仇敵來將稗子種撒在麥子裏就去了到長苗結穗的時候稗子也現出來地主的僕人來告訴說主阿你不是撒好種在田裏麼怎麼有這稗子呢主人說這是仇敵作的僕人說、你要我們去拔除麼、

ST. MATTHEW.

29 But he said, Nay; lest while ye gather up the tares, ye root up also the wheat with them.

30 Let both grow together until the harvest: and in the time of harvest I will say to the reapers, Gather ye together first the tares, and bind them in bundles to burn them: but gather the wheat into my barn.

31 ¶ Another parable put he forth unto them, saying, The kingdom of heaven is like to a grain of mustard seed, which a man took, and sowed in his field:

32 Which indeed is the least of all seeds: but when it is grown, it is the greatest among herbs, and becometh a tree, so that the birds of the air come and lodge in the branches thereof.

33 ¶ Another parable spake he unto them; The kingdom of heaven is like unto leaven, which a woman took, and hid in three measures of meal, till the whole was leavened.

34 All these things spake Jesus unto the multitude in parables; and without a parable spake he not unto them:

35 That it might be fulfilled which was spoken by the prophet, saying, I will open my mouth in parables; I will utter things which have been kept secret from the foundation of the world.

主人說、不要、恐怕拔除稗子、連麥子也拔出來。容這兩樣一齊長、等著收割、到了收割的時候、我告訴割麥子的、先將稗子拔除捆成捆留著燒後將麥子收在倉裏。○又設一個比喻對衆人說、天國如同一粒芥菜種被人種在田裏、這是百種中最小的、等到長成了、比各樣菜都大、成了樹空中的雀鳥飛來、住在他的枝上。○又對他們講一個比喻說、天國如同麪酵婦人拏來搁在三斗麪裏、麪就都發起來了、這都是耶穌用比喻對衆人說的話、不是比喻不對他們說、正應了先知所說的話、說我開口就說比喻的話將創世以來所隱藏的都講明了。

36 Then Jesus sent the multitude away, and went into the house: and his disciples came unto him, saying, Declare unto us the parable of the tares of the field.

37 He answered and said unto them, He that soweth the good seed is the Son of man;

38 The field is the world; the good seed are the children of the kingdom; but the tares are the children of the wicked one;

39 The enemy that sowed them is the devil; the harvest is the end of the world; and the reapers are the angels.

40 As therefore the tares are gathered and burned in the fire; so shall it be in the end of this world.

41 The Son of man shall send forth his angels, and they shall gather out of his kingdom all things that offend, and them which do iniquity;

42 And shall cast them into a furnace of fire: there shall be wailing and gnashing of teeth.

43 Then shall the righteous shine forth as the sun in the kingdom of their Father. Who hath ears to hear, let him hear.

44 ¶ Again, the kingdom of heaven is like unto treasure hid in a field; the which when a man hath found, he hideth, and for joy thereof goeth and selleth all that he hath, and buyeth that field.

○當下耶穌遣散了衆人、進了房子、門徒進前來說、請將田間稗子的比喻講給我們聽。耶穌對他們說、那撒好種的就是人子、那田地就是世界、好種就是天國的子民、稗子就是那惡魔的種類、撒稗子的仇敵就是魔鬼、收割的時候就是世界的末日、收割的人就是天使。把稗子聚起來用火焚燒這世界的末日也是如此、人子將要差遣他的使者將凡陷人在罪裏的和作惡的人從他的國裏挑揀出來、丟在火爐裏、在那裏必要哀哭切齒了。那時義人在他們父的國裏有光彩、如同日頭一般。凡有耳可聽的都應當聽。○天國又如寶貝藏在田地裏、人遇見了、就隱瞞著歡歡喜喜的去賣了他所有的買這塊田地。

ST. MATTHEW.

45 ¶ Again, the kingdom of heaven is like unto a merchantman, seeking goodly pearls:

46 Who, when he had found one pearl of great price, went and sold all that he had, and bought it.

47 ¶ Again, the kingdom of heaven is like unto a net, that was cast into the sea, and gathered of every kind:

48 Which, when it was full, they drew to shore, and sat down, and gathered the good into vessels, but cast the bad away.

49 So shall it be at the end of the world: the angels shall come forth, and sever the wicked from among the just,

50 And shall cast them into the furnace of fire; there shall be wailing and gnashing of teeth.

51 Jesus saith unto them, Have ye understood all these things? They say unto him, Yea, Lord.

52 Then said he unto them, Therefore every scribe *which is* instructed unto the kingdom of heaven, is like unto a man *that is* a householder, which bringeth forth out of his treasure *things* new and old.

53 ¶ And it came to pass, *that* when Jesus had finished these parables, he departed thence.

○天國又如買寶人尋找好珠子、遇見一顆重價的珠子、就去賣了他所有的買這顆珠子。○天國又如同網撒在海裏聚集各樣水族滿了人就拉到岸上來坐下揀好的收在器皿裏將不好的丟棄了世界的末日也是如此天使出來從義人中將惡人分別出來、丟在火窰裏、在那裏必要哀哭切齒了。耶穌問他們說、這話你們都明白麼他們說、主我們明白了。耶穌說、所以凡讀書人學問能通達天國道理的、就如一個家主、從他庫裏拏出新舊的東西來。○耶穌說完這些比喻就離了那裏、

54 And when he was come into his own country, he taught them in their synagogue, insomuch that they were astonished, and said, Whence hath this *man* this wisdom, and *these* mighty works?

55 Is not this the carpenter's son? is not his mother called Mary? and his brethren, James, and Joses, and Simon, and Judas?

56 And his sisters, are they not all with us? Whence then hath this *man* all these things?

57 And they were offended in him. But Jesus said unto them, A prophet is not without honour, save in his own country, and in his own house.

58 And he did not many mighty works there because of their unbelief.

CHAPTER 14.

AT that time Herod the tetrarch heard of the fame of Jesus,

2 And said unto his servants, This is John the Baptist; he is risen from the dead; and therefore mighty works do shew forth themselves in him.

囘到家鄉、在會堂裏教訓那裏的人、他們都詫異說這人如何有這樣的智慧這樣的異能呢、他不是木匠的兒子麼他母親不是名叫馬利亞麼他弟兄不是雅各約西西門猶大麼他姐妹不是都住在我們這裏麼這人如何能這樣呢、他們就厭棄他耶穌對他們說大凡先知除了本地本家之外、沒有不被人尊敬的、耶穌因為他們不信、就在那裏不多行奇事了。

第十四章

那時候分封的王希律聽見耶穌的聲名、就對他臣子說、這必是施洗的約翰從死裏復活所以能行這些奇事。

ST. MATTHEW.

3 ¶ For Herod had laid hold on John, and bound him, and put *him* in prison for Herodias' sake, his brother Philip's wife.

4 For John said unto him, It is not lawful for thee to have her.

5 And when he would have put him to death, he feared the multitude, because they counted him as a prophet.

6 But when Herod's birthday was kept, the daughter of Herodias danced before them, and pleased Herod.

7 Whereupon he promised with an oath to give her whatsoever she would ask.

8 And she, being before instructed of her mother, said, Give me here John Baptist's head in a charger.

9 And the king was sorry: nevertheless for the oath's sake, and them which sat with him at meat, he commanded *it* to be given her.

10 And he sent, and beheaded John in the prison.

11 And his head was brought in a charger, and given to the damsel: and she brought *it* to her mother.

12 And his disciples came, and took up the body, and buried it, and went and told Jesus.

馬太第十四章

³先是希律爲他兄弟腓力的妻子希羅底的緣故、將約翰鎖拏下監。因爲約翰曾向希律說、你娶這婦人、是不合理的⁵希律就要殺他、只是懼怕百姓、因爲百姓尊約翰爲先知。⁶怡遇希律的生日、希羅底的女兒在衆人面前跳舞、希律歡喜就起誓應許他隨他所求的賜給他。⁸他聽了母親的囑咐、便求希律說、請將施洗約翰的頭、放在盤子裏賜我。⁹王就憂愁無奈已經起了誓、並且同席的人都在那裏、於是盼咐給他。¹⁰打發人到監裏斬了約翰的頭、放在盤子裏給了女子、女子送給他母親。¹¹約翰的門徒來收他的屍首葬埋了、就去告訴耶穌。

13 ¶ When Jesus heard *of it*, he departed thence by ship into a desert place apart: and when the people had heard *thereof*, they followed him on foot out of the cities.

14 And Jesus went forth, and saw a great multitude, and was moved with compassion toward them, and he healed their sick.

15 ¶ And when it was evening, his disciples came to him, saying, This is a desert place, and the time is now past; send the multitude away, that they may go into the villages, and buy themselves victuals.

16 But Jesus said unto them, They need not depart; give ye them to eat.

17 And they say unto him, We have here but five loaves, and two fishes.

18 He said, Bring them hither to me.

19 And he commanded the multitude to sit down on the grass, and took the five loaves, and the two fishes, and looking up to heaven, he blessed, and brake, and gave the loaves to *his* disciples, and the disciples to the multitude.

20 And they did all eat, and were filled: and they took up of the fragments that remained twelve baskets full.

21 And they that had eaten were about five thousand men, beside women and children.

耶穌聽見了、就上船離開那地方、獨自往野地裏去。眾人聽見、都從各城裏步行跟隨他。○耶穌出來、看見許多的人、就憐恤他們、醫好他們中間的病人。天將晚的時候、門徒進前來說、這是野地、天已經晚了、請遣散眾人、叫他們往村子裏去買東西喫。耶穌說、不用他們去、你們給他們喫罷。門徒說、我們這裏只有五個餅、兩尾魚。耶穌說、拏來給我。就吩咐眾人坐在草地上、拏著五個餅、兩尾魚、望著天祝謝了、擘開餅、遞給門徒、門徒分給眾人。眾人都喫飽了、收拾賸下的零碎、盛滿了十二筐子。喫的人、除了婦人孩子、約有五千。

St. MATTHEW.

22 ¶ And straightway Jesus constrained his disciples to get into a ship, and to go before him unto the other side, while he sent the multitudes away.

23 ¶ And when he had sent the multitudes away, he went up into a mountain apart to pray: and when the evening was come, he was there alone,

24 But the ship was now in the midst of the sea, tossed with waves: for the wind was contrary.

25 And in the fourth watch of the night Jesus went unto them, walking on the sea.

26 And when the disciples saw him walking on the sea, they were troubled, saying, It is a spirit; and they cried out for fear.

27 But straightway Jesus spake unto them, saying, Be of good cheer; it is I; be not afraid.

28 And Peter answered him and said, Lord, if it be thou, bid me come unto thee on the water.

29 And he said, Come. And when Peter was come down out of the ship, he walked on the water, to go to Jesus.

30 But when he saw the wind boisterous, he was afraid; and beginning to sink, he cried, saying, Lord, save me.

○耶穌要遣散眾人、就催門徒上船、先渡到那邊岸上去。眾人散後耶穌獨自上山祈禱、天就黑了、只有耶穌一人在那裏。船在海中、因為風不順、被波浪搖動夜裏四更時分耶穌在海面上行走、徃門徒那裏去門徒看見耶穌在海面上行走、就驚慌了、說這必是怪物、就懼怕喊叫起來耶穌急忙對他們說、你們放心、是我、不要懼怕。彼得說果然是　主、請呌我也從水面上走到你那裏去。主救我也從水面上行走要到耶穌那裏去見風甚大就懼怕將要沉下去、喊叫說、　主救我。

58 ST. MATTHEW.

31 And immediately Jesus stretched forth *his* hand, and caught him, and said unto him, O thou of little faith, wherefore didst thou doubt?

32 And when they were come into the ship, the wind ceased.

33 Then they that were in the ship came and worshipped him, saying, Of a truth thou art the Son of God.

34 ¶ And when they were gone over, they came into the land of Gennesaret.

35 And when the men of that place had knowledge of him, they sent out into all that country round about, and brought unto him all that were diseased;

36 And besought him that they might only touch the hem of his garment: and as many as touched were made perfectly whole.

CHAPTER 15.

THEN came to Jesus scribes and Pharisees, which were of Jerusalem, saying,

2 Why do thy disciples transgress the tradition of the elders? for they wash not their hands when they eat bread.

3 But he answered and said unto them, Why do ye also transgress the commandment of God by your tradition?

馬太第十五章

耶穌伸手拉住他、說、你這小信的人爲甚麼疑惑呢。一上了船、風就息了。在船上的人都來拜耶穌、說你實在是　神的兒子了。〇耶穌和門徒過了海到了革尼撒勒的地界那裏的人認識耶穌就打發人到周圍地方去報信有人將那裏所有的病人帶來見耶穌只求耶穌准他們摸耶穌的衣裳穗子、摸著的人、就都好了。

第十五章

那時候有耶路撒冷的讀書人、和法利賽人、來見耶穌說、你的門徒爲甚麼犯了從古人傳下來的規矩喫飯的時候不洗手呢。耶穌囘答說、你們爲甚麼因爲那傳下來的規矩犯了　神的誡呢。

ST. MATTHEW.

4 For God commanded, saying, Honour thy father and mother: and, He that curseth father or mother, let him die the death.

5 But ye say, Whosoever shall say to *his* father or *his* mother, *It is* a gift, by whatsoever thou mightest be profited by me;

6 And honour not his father or his mother, *he shall be free.* Thus have ye made the commandment of God of none effect by your tradition.

7 *Ye* hypocrites, well did Esaias prophesy of you, saying,

8 This people draweth nigh unto me with their mouth, and honoureth me with *their* lips; but their heart is far from me.

9 But in vain they do worship me, teaching *for* doctrines the commandments of men.

10 ¶ And he called the multitude, and said unto them, Hear, and understand:

11 Not that which goeth into the mouth defileth a man; but that which cometh out of the mouth, this defileth a man.

12 Then came his disciples, and said unto him, Knowest thou that the Pharisees were offended, after they heard this saying?

13 But he answered and said, Every plant, which my heavenly Father hath not planted, shall be rooted up.

神吩說應當孝敬父母又說呪罵父母的必當治死他你們倒說人若對父母說、我所當奉給你的已經作了禮物以後不孝敬父母是可以的這就是你們守著所傳下來的規矩廢了 神的誡了、假冒為善的人以賽亞預先指著你們說的話、是不錯的他說這百姓用口親近我他用唇尊敬我他們的心卻是遠離我他們將人所吩附的當作道理教訓人所以拜我也是枉然耶穌叫了眾人來對他們說你們要聽要明白不是入口的能污穢人乃是出口的能污穢人耶穌回答說凡栽種的物若不是我天父栽種的必要拔出他的根來。聽見這話甚不喜悅你知道麼耶穌回答說凡栽種的物若不是我天父栽種的必

ST. MATTHEW.

14 Let them alone: they be blind leaders of the blind. And if the blind lead the blind, both shall fall into the ditch.

15 Then answered Peter and said unto him, Declare unto us this parable.

16 And Jesus said, Are ye also yet without understanding?

17 Do not ye yet understand, that whatsoever entereth in at the mouth goeth into the belly, and is cast out into the draught?

18 But those things which proceed out of the mouth come forth from the heart; and they defile the man.

19 For out of the heart proceed evil thoughts, murders, adulteries, fornications, thefts, false witness, blasphemies:

20 These are *the things* which defile a man: but to eat with unwashen hands defileth not a man.

21 ¶ Then Jesus went thence, and departed into the coasts of Tyre and Sidon.

22 And, behold, a woman of Canaan came out of the same coasts, and cried unto him, saying, Have mercy on me, O Lord, *thou* Son of David; my daughter is grievously vexed with a devil.

馬太第十五章

十四 任憑他們罷、他們是瞎子領瞎子、若是瞎子領瞎子、兩個人必都要掉在坑裏彼得

十五 說、請將這個比喻講給我們聽耶穌

十六 說、你們也不明白麼、豈不知凡入口的運化在

十七 肚裏終久落在茅廁裏麼、惟有出口的、是從心裏發的這纔能污穢人像那惡念兇

十八 殺姦淫苟合盜竊妄證謗讟這都是從心裏發的都能污穢人、若是不洗手喫飯那

二十 不能污穢人。○耶穌離開那地方、往推羅西頓的境內去有一個迦南的婦人從那

二十二 地方出來、大聲求耶穌說、主大衞的子孫、憐憫我、我的女兒被鬼附著甚苦。

ST. MATTHEW.

23 But he answered her not a word. And his disciples came and besought him, saying, Send her away; for she crieth after us.

24 But he answered and said, I am not sent but unto the lost sheep of the house of Israel.

25 Then came she and worshipped him, saying, Lord, help me.

26 But he answered and said, It is not meet to take the children's bread, and to cast *it* to dogs.

27 And she said, Truth, Lord: yet the dogs eat of the crumbs which fall from their masters' table.

28 Then Jesus answered and said unto her, O woman, great is thy faith: be it unto thee even as thou wilt. And her daughter was made whole from that very hour.

29 And Jesus departed from thence, and came nigh unto the sea of Galilee; and went up into a mountain, and sat down there.

30 And great multitudes came unto him, having with them *those that were* lame, blind, dumb, maimed, and many others, and cast them down at Jesus' feet; and he healed them:

耶穌一言不答、徒進前來、求耶穌說、他在我們後面喊叫、請叫他去罷。耶穌回答說、我奉差遣而來、只爲以色列族迷失的羊。婦人來拜耶穌說、求　主拯救耶穌回答說、將兒女的餅丟給狗喫、是不可以的。婦人說、　主阿、是的、但是狗也喫他主人棹子底下所掉的零碎耶穌說婦人你的信是大的、照你所願意的與你成全了罷。從這時候他女兒就好了。○耶穌離開那地方、到了加利利的海邊上山坐下有許多的人到他面前來帶著瘸腿的瞎眼的啞吧、有殘疾的、和各樣的病人放在耶穌的脚下、耶穌就醫好他們。

31 Insomuch that the multitude wondered, when they saw the dumb to speak, the maimed to be whole, the lame to walk, and the blind to see: and they glorified the God of Israel.

32 ¶ Then Jesus called his disciples *unto him*, and said, I have compassion on the multitude, because they continue with me now three days, and have nothing to eat: and I will not send them away fasting, lest they faint in the way.

33 And his disciples say unto him, Whence should we have so much bread in the wilderness, as to fill so great a multitude?

34 And Jesus saith unto them, How many loaves have ye? And they said, Seven, and a few little fishes.

35 And he commanded the multitude to sit down on the ground.

36 And he took the seven loaves and the fishes, and gave thanks, and brake *them*, and gave to his disciples, and the disciples to the multitude.

37 And they did all eat, and were filled: and they took up of the broken *meat* that was left seven baskets full.

38 And they that did eat were four thousand men, beside women and children.

39 And he sent away the multitude, and took ship, and came into the coasts of Magdala.

CHAPTER 16.

THE Pharisees also with the Sadducees came, and tempting desired him that he would shew them a sign from heaven.

2 He answered and said unto them, When it is evening, ye say, It *will be* fair weather: for the sky is red.

3 And in the morning, *It will be* foul weather to day: for the sky is red and lowering. O *ye* hypocrites, ye can discern the face of the sky; but can ye not *discern* the signs of the times?

4 A wicked and adulterous generation seeketh after a sign; and there shall no sign be given unto it, but the sign of the prophet Jonas. And he left them, and departed.

5 And when his disciples were come to the other side, they had forgotten to take bread.

6 ¶ Then Jesus said unto them, Take heed and beware of the leaven of the Pharisees and of the Sadducees.

7 And they reasoned among themselves, saying, It is because we have taken no bread.

8 *Which* when Jesus perceived, he said unto them, O ye of little faith, why reason ye among yourselves, because ye have brought no bread?

第十六章

法利賽和撒都該人、來試探耶穌、請耶穌從天上顯奇事與他們看。二耶穌回答說、晚上天有紅光你們就說天必要晴、早晨天紅了又發昏暗、你們就說、今日必有風雨、假冒爲善的人天上的氣色你們尚且能辨別、倒不明白這時候的奇事麽奸惡的世代要看奇事、除了先知約拏的那件奇事、再沒有奇事給你們看。耶穌就離開他們去了。○門徒渡到那邊岸上忘了拏餅耶穌對他們說、你們謹防法利賽和撒都該人的酵、門徒彼此議論說這是因爲我們沒有拏餅彼此議論呢。八耶穌知道對他們說你們這小信的人爲甚麽因爲沒有拏餅彼此議論呢。

64 ST. MATTHEW.

9 Do ye not yet understand, neither remember the five thousand, and how many baskets ye took up?

10 Neither the seven loaves of the four thousand, and how many baskets ye took up?

11 How is it that ye do not understand that I spake *it* not to you concerning bread, that ye should beware of the leaven of the Pharisees and of the Sadducees?

12 Then understood they how that he bade *them* not beware of the leaven of bread, but of the doctrine of the Pharisees and of the Sadducees.

13 ¶ When Jesus came into the coasts of Cesarea Philippi, he asked his disciples, saying, Whom do men say that I, the Son of man, am?

14 And they said, Some *say that thou art* John the Baptist; some, Elias; and others Jeremias, or one of the prophets.

15 He saith unto them, But whom say ye that I am?

16 And Simon Peter answered and said, Thou art the Christ, the Son of the living God.

17 And Jesus answered and said unto him, Blessed art thou, Simon Bar-jona: for flesh and blood hath not revealed *it* unto thee, but my Father which is in heaven.

馬太第十六章

你們還不省悟麼五個餅分給五千人又收拾了幾筐子零碎你們不記得麼七個餅分給四千人又收拾了幾籃子零碎你們不記得麼我告訴你們該謹防法利賽和撒都該人的酵這話不是指著餅說的你們怎麼不明白呢門徒這纔明白耶穌到了該撒利亞腓力比的境內問門徒說人說我人子是誰有人說是施洗的約翰有人說是以利亞又有人說是耶利米或是先知裏的一位耶穌說你們說我是誰西門彼得說你是基督是永生　神的兒子耶穌說西門巴爾約拏你是有福的因為這不是世上的人指示給你的乃是我在天上的父指示的

ST. MATTHEW.

18 And I say also unto thee, That thou art Peter, and upon this rock I will build my church; and the gates of hell shall not prevail against it.

19 And I will give unto thee the keys of the kingdom of heaven: and whatsoever thou shalt bind on earth shall be bound in heaven; and whatsoever thou shalt loose on earth shall be loosed in heaven.

20 Then charged he his disciples that they should tell no man that he was Jesus the Christ.

21 ¶ From that time forth began Jesus to shew unto his disciples, how that he must go unto Jerusalem, and suffer many things of the elders and chief priests and scribes, and be killed, and be raised again the third day.

22 Then Peter took him, and began to rebuke him, saying, Be it far from thee, Lord: this shall not be unto thee.

23 But he turned, and said unto Peter, Get thee behind me, Satan: thou art an offence unto me: for thou savourest not the things that be of God, but those that be of men.

24 ¶ Then said Jesus unto his disciples, If any *man* will come after me, let him deny himself, and take up his cross, and follow me.

我又告訴你、你是彼得、彼得即磐石之意 我要立我的敎會在這磐石上、陰間的權柄不能勝他。我並且要將天國的鑰匙賜給你、凡你在地上所捆綁的、在天上也要捆綁、在地上所釋放的、在天上也要釋放。於是耶穌吩咐門徒、不可告訴人、耶穌是基督。○從此耶穌指示門徒、自己必須上耶路撒冷去、在那裏受長老祭司長和士子許多的苦、並且被殺第三日復活 彼得就拉著他勸他說主這是萬不可的也不至於如此。耶穌轉身對彼得說撒但退去罷、你是阻擋我的、你不體貼 神的意思只體貼人的意思。耶穌對門徒說有人要跟從我就當克己背著十字架跟從我、

25 For whosoever will save his life shall lose it: and whosoever will lose his life for my sake shall find it.

26 For what is a man profited, if he shall gain the world, and lose his own soul? or what shall a man give in exchange for his soul?

27 For the Son of man shall come in the glory of his Father with his angels; and then he shall reward every man according to his works.

28 Verily I say unto you, There be some standing here, which shall not taste of death, till they see the Son of man coming in his kingdom.

CHAPTER 17.

AND after six days Jesus taketh Peter, James, and John his brother, and bringeth them up into a high mountain apart,

2 And was transfigured before them: and his face did shine as the sun, and his raiment was white as the light.

3 And, behold, there appeared unto them Moses and Elias talking with him.

凡要保全生命的必要喪掉生命、喪掉生命或作喪掉靈魂有甚麽益處人能挈甚麽換生命或作靈魂呢、人子必得著天父的榮耀同著衆天使降臨那時候必要照著各人的行爲報應他、我實在告訴你們、站在這裏的有人在未死以前必要看見人子降臨在他國裏。

第十七章

過了六日耶穌帶著彼得雅各和雅各的兄弟約翰暗暗的上了高山、耶穌在他們面前變了形像、臉而明亮如日頭、衣裳潔白放光、忽有摩西以利亞顯現在他們面前和耶穌說話。

ST. MATTHEW.

4 Then answered Peter, and said unto Jesus, Lord, it is good for us to be here: if thou wilt, let us make here three tabernacles; one for thee, and one for Moses, and one for Elias.

5 While he yet spake, behold, a bright cloud overshadowed them: and behold a voice out of the cloud, which said, This is my beloved Son, in whom I am well pleased; hear ye him.

6 And when the disciples heard it, they fell on their face, and were sore afraid.

7 And Jesus came and touched them, and said, Arise, and be not afraid.

8 And when they had lifted up their eyes, they saw no man, save Jesus only.

9 And as they came down from the mountain, Jesus charged them, saying, Tell the vision to no man, until the Son of man be risen again from the dead.

10 And his disciples asked him, saying, Why then say the scribes that Elias must first come?

11 And Jesus answered and said unto them, Elias truly shall first come, and restore all things.

12 But I say unto you, that Elias is come already, and they knew him not, but have done unto him whatsoever they listed. Likewise shall also the Son of man suffer of them.

彼得對耶穌說、主、我們在這裏最好、你若願意、我們就在這裏搭三座棚、一座為你、一座為摩西、一座為以利亞、說話之間、有光明的雲遮住他們、有聲音從雲裏出來、說、這是我的愛子、我所喜悅的、你們應當聽他。門徒聽見就俯伏在地、懼怕得很。耶穌進前摸他們說你們起來、不要懼怕。門徒舉目觀看不見一人、只有耶穌在那裏。○下山的時候、耶穌吩咐他們說、人子還沒有從死裏復活、你們不可將所看見的告訴人。門徒問耶穌說、讀書人為甚麼說以利亞必要先來。耶穌回答說、以利亞自然先來、整理萬事。我告訴你們、以利亞已經來了、人都不認識、任意待他這樣、人子也要受他們的害。

13 Then the disciples understood that he spake unto them of John the Baptist.

14 ¶ And when they were come to the multitude, there came to him a *certain* man, kneeling down to him, and saying,

15 Lord, have mercy on my son; for he is lunatic, and sore vexed: for ofttimes he falleth into the fire, and oft into the water.

16 And I brought him to thy disciples, and they could not cure him.

17 Then Jesus answered and said, O faithless and perverse generation, how long shall I be with you? how long shall I suffer you? bring him hither to me.

18 And Jesus rebuked the devil; and he departed out of him: and the child was cured from that very hour.

19 Then came the disciples to Jesus apart, and said, Why could not we cast him out?

20 And Jesus said unto them, Because of your unbelief: for verily I say unto you, If ye have faith as a grain of mustard seed, ye shall say unto this mountain, Remove hence to yonder place; and it shall remove: and nothing shall be impossible unto you.

21 Howbeit this kind goeth not out but by prayer and fasting.

門徒這纔明白耶穌所說的、是指著施洗的約翰。○到了眾人那裏有人來到耶穌面前跪下說主憐恤我的兒子他害顛癇的病甚苦、屢次跌在火裏屢次跌在水裏、我帶他到你門徒那裏他們不能醫治這裏到幾時呢帶他到我這裏來耶穌回答說這悖逆不信的世代、我在你們這裏到幾時呢我忍耐你們到幾時呢帶他到我這裏來耶穌指斥那鬼、鬼就出去、那人的兒子立刻好了門徒暗暗的到耶穌面前來說我們不能逐出那鬼、是甚麼緣故耶穌說因為你們不信、我實在告訴你們、若有芥菜種那樣大的信心、就是吩咐這座山從這邊挪移到那邊也必挪移並且你們沒有一件不能作的事了。至於那一類的鬼若不禱告禁食就不能趕他出去。

22 ¶ And while they abode in Galilee, Jesus said unto them, The Son of man shall be betrayed into the hands of men:

23 And they shall kill him, and the third day he shall be raised again. And they were exceeding sorry.

24 ¶ And when they were come to Capernaum, they that received tribute *money* came to Peter, and said, Doth not your Master pay tribute?

25 He saith, Yes. And when he was come into the house, Jesus prevented him, saying, What thinkest thou, Simon? of whom do the kings of the earth take custom or tribute? of their own children, or of strangers?

26 Peter saith unto him, Of strangers. Jesus saith unto him, Then are the children free.

27 Notwithstanding, lest we should offend them, go thou to the sea, and cast a hook, and take up the fish that first cometh up; and when thou hast opened his mouth, thou shalt find a piece of money: that take, and give them for me and thee.

○耶穌周流加利利的時候、對門徒說、人子將要被賣在人手裏、被他們殺害、第三日必要復活、門徒就大大的憂愁。○到了迦百農、有為聖殿收稅的人來、對彼得說、你們先生納稅不納、彼得說納稅、彼得進了屋子、耶穌先向他說、西門你的意思怎樣、世上各國的王、向誰徵收關稅丁稅、是向自己的兒子呢、還是向外人呢。彼得說、向外人徵收、耶穌說、既然如此、兒子就可免稅了、但恐怕惹他們不喜悅你、且往海邊去釣魚、將先釣上來的魚取來開了他的口、可以得一塊銀錢、拏去給他們、作你我的稅銀。

CHAPTER 18.

AT the same time came the disciples unto Jesus, saying, Who is the greatest in the kingdom of heaven?

2 And Jesus called a little child unto him, and set him in the midst of them,

3 And said, Verily I say unto you, Except ye be converted, and become as little children, ye shall not enter into the kingdom of heaven.

4 Whosoever therefore shall humble himself as this little child, the same is greatest in the kingdom of heaven.

5 And whoso shall receive one such little child in my name receivth me.

6 But whoso shall offend one of these little ones which believe in me, it were better for him that a millstone were hanged about his neck, and *that* he were drowned in the depth of the sea.

7 ¶ Woe unto the world because of offences! for it must needs be that offences come; but woe to that man by whom the offence cometh!

第十八章

一那時候門徒進前來、問耶穌說天國裏誰是最大的。二耶穌叫一個孩子來、使他站在他們中間、說我實在告訴你們、你們若不改變氣質、不像小孩子就不能進天國裏去。所以凡自己謙卑像這小孩子的、他在天國就是最大的、凡爲我的名接待一像這小孩子的、就是接待我了。凡叫這信我的一个小子陷在罪裏的、這人倒不如早有人將磨盤石拴在他的頸項上、沈在深海裏這世界是有禍的、因爲陷人在罪裏陷人在罪裏固然是不能免的事、只是陷人在罪的人是有禍的。

ST. MATTHEW.

8 Wherefore if thy hand or thy foot offend thee, cut them off, and cast *them* from thee: it is better for thee to enter into life halt or maimed, rather than having two hands or two feet to be cast into everlasting fire.

9 And if thine eye offend thee, pluck it out, and cast *it* from thee: it is better for thee to enter into life with one eye, rather than having two eyes to be cast into hell fire.

10 Take heed that ye despise not one of these little ones; for I say unto you, That in heaven their angels do always behold the face of my Father which is in heaven.

11 For the Son of man is come to save that which was lost.

12 How think ye? if a man have a hundred sheep, and one of them be gone astray, doth he not leave the ninety and nine, and goeth into the mountains, and seeketh that which is gone astray?

13 And if so be that he find it, verily I say unto you, he rejoiceth more of that *sheep*, than of the ninety and nine which went not astray.

14 Even so it is not the will of your Father which is in heaven, that one of these little ones should perish.

倘若你一隻手、一隻脚、叫你犯罪、就砍下來丟掉、你短一手一脚進入永生、強如有兩手兩脚被投在永火裏。倘若你的眼睛叫你犯罪、就剜出來丟掉、你短一隻眼進入永生、強如有兩隻眼被投在地獄的火裏。○你們要小心、不可輕看這小子裏的一個我告訴你們、他們的天使在天上、常見我天父的面八子來、特爲要救喪亡的人。比如一個人有一百隻羊迷失了一隻你們的意思如何那個人豈不是撇下這九十九隻在山上尋找那一隻迷失的羊去麼若是找著了、我實在告訴你們、他爲這一隻羊歡喜比爲那沒有迷失的九十九隻羊歡喜還大呢。如此、你們天父也不願這小子裏迷失一個。

ST. MATTHEW.

15 ¶ Moreover if thy brother shall trespass against thee, go and tell him his fault between thee and him alone: if he shall hear thee, thou hast gained thy brother.

16 But if he will not hear *thee, then* take with thee one or two more, that in the mouth of two or three witnesses every word may be established.

17 And if he shall neglect to hear them, tell *it* unto the church: but if he neglect to hear the church, let him be unto thee as a heathen man and a publican.

18 Verily I say unto you, Whatsoever ye shall bind on earth shall be bound in heaven; and whatsoever ye shall loose on earth shall be loosed in heaven.

19 Again I say unto you, That if two of you shall agree on earth as touching any thing that they shall ask, it shall be done for them of my Father which is in heaven.

20 For where two or three are gathered together in my name, there am I in the midst of them.

21 ¶ Then came Peter to him, and said, Lord, how oft shall my brother sin against me, and I forgive him? till seven times?

馬太第十八章

○倘若兄弟得罪你、你就去在背地裏責備他、他若聽從你、就是你救了你兄弟了。若不聽從你、就帶一兩個人同去、因爲無論甚麼事必憑著兩三人的口作見證方能定局。若不聽從他們、就告訴敎會、若不聽從敎會、就將他看作外邦人和稅吏一樣。我實在告訴你們、凡你們在地上所捆綁的、在天上也要捆綁、在地上所釋放的、在天上也要釋放。我又告訴你們、若你們中間有兩個人在地上同心合意的求甚麼事、我在天上的父必爲他們成全。因爲無論在何處有兩三人奉我的名聚會我必在他們中間。○那時候彼得進前來問耶穌說主兄弟得罪我、我應當饒恕他幾次、到七次可以麽。

ST. MATTHEW.

22 Jesus saith unto him, I say not unto thee, Until seven times: but, Until seventy times seven.

23 ¶ Therefore is the kingdom of heaven likened unto a certain king, which would take account of his servants.

24 And when he had begun to reckon, one was brought unto him, which owed him ten thousand talents.

25 But forasmuch as he had not to pay, his lord commanded him to be sold, and his wife, and children, and all that he had, and payment to be made.

26 The servant therefore fell down, and worshipped him, saying, Lord, have patience with me, and I will pay thee all.

27 Then the lord of that servant was moved with compassion, and loosed him, and forgave him the debt.

28 But the same servant went out, and found one of his fellow servants, which owed him a hundred pence: and he laid hands on him, and took *him* by the throat, saying, Pay me that thou owest.

29 And his fellow servant fell down at his feet, and besought him, saying, Have patience with me, and I will pay thee all.

30 And he would not: but went and cast him into prison, till he should pay the debt.

耶穌對他說、我說不是到七次、乃是到七十個七次。天國如同君王、要和他的僕人算賬算的時候、有人帶一個欠一千萬銀的進前來、因為他無力償還他主人吩咐將他和他的妻子兒女同他所有的都賣了賠還那僕人俯伏拜他說請主寬容我、我將來必都還清他主人就憐憫他、將他釋放並且豁免他的債那僕人出來、遇見一個同伴欠他十兩銀子、那僕人就揪住他掐他的喉嚨、說、你欠我的還我。同伴俯伏在他面前求他說、請你寬容我、我將來必要還清他不應允、就將他下了監、等他還清了所欠的債。

31 So when his fellow servants saw what was done, they were very sorry, and came and told unto their lord all that was done.

32 Then his lord, after that he had called him, said unto him, O thou wicked servant, I forgave thee all that debt, because thou desiredst me:

33 Shouldest not thou also have had compassion on thy fellow servant, even as I had pity on thee?

34 And his lord was wroth, and delivered him to the tormentors, till he should pay all that was due unto him.

35 So likewise shall my heavenly Father do also unto you, if ye from your hearts forgive not every one his brother their trespasses.

CHAPTER 19.

AND it came to pass, *that* when Jesus had finished these sayings, he departed from Galilee, and came into the coasts of Judea beyond Jordan;

2 And great multitudes followed him; and he healed them there.

3 ¶ The Pharisees also came unto him, tempting him, and saying unto him, Is it lawful for a man to put away his wife for every cause?

馬太第十九章

三一他的衆同伴、看見這事、很不歡喜將這事告訴了主人。主人將他叫了來、說、你這惡奴、你求我、我就將你所欠的都豁免了、你不應當憐恤你的同伴像我憐恤你麼。主人就發怒將他交給獄官等他還清了所欠的債。你們各人若不誠心饒恕弟兄的過犯、我天父也必要如此待你們了。

第十九章

耶穌說完這話就離開加利利、到了猶太境界約但河外。有許多人跟隨他、耶穌在那裏醫好他們中間的病人有法利賽人來試探耶穌說、人無論甚麼緣故都可以休妻麼。

ST. MATTHEW.

4 And he answered and said unto them, Have ye not read, that he which made *them* at the beginning made them male and female,

5 And said, For this cause shall a man leave father and mother, and shall cleave to his wife: and they twain shall be one flesh?

6 Wherefore they are no more twain, but one flesh. What therefore God hath joined together, let not man put asunder.

7 They say unto him, Why did Moses then command to give a writing of divorcement, and to put her away?

8 He saith unto them, Moses because of the hardness of your hearts suffered you to put away your wives: but from the beginning it was not so.

9 And I say unto you, Whosoever shall put away his wife, except *it be* for fornication, and shall marry another, committeth adultery: and whoso marrieth her which is put away doth commit adultery.

10 ¶ His disciples say unto him, If the case of the man be so with *his* wife, it is not good to marry.

11 But he said unto them, All *men* cannot receive this saying, save *they* to whom it is given.

耶穌回答說造萬物的主起初造人、是造一男一女並且說因此人離開父母與妻子如膠似漆兩人成爲一體這經你沒有讀過麼、這樣看來夫妻不算兩個人、乃是一體的了、所以　神配合的、人不可分開他們說、這樣、摩西叉爲甚麼吩附我們立了休書繞可以休妻呢、耶穌說摩西因爲你們心太忍所以容你們休妻但起初不是這樣、我告訴你們、若不是爲淫亂的緣故休妻另娶、就是犯了姦淫了、有人娶被休的女人也是犯了姦淫了、門徒對耶穌說人和妻子旣是這樣、倒不如不娶。耶穌說人不能都聽受這話、惟有禀賦這樣性情的人纔能聽受。

12 For there are some eunuchs, which were so born from *their* mother's womb: and there are some eunuchs, which were made eunuchs of men: and there be eunuchs, which have made themselves eunuchs for the kingdom of heaven's sake. He that is able to receive *it*, let him receive *it*.

13 ¶ Then were there brought unto him little children, that he should put *his* hands on them, and pray: and the disciples rebuked them.

14 But Jesus said, Suffer little children, and forbid them not, to come unto me; for of such is the kingdom of heaven.

15 And he laid *his* hands on them, and departed thence.

16 ¶ And, behold, one came and said unto him, Good Master, what good thing shall I do, that I may have eternal life?

17 And he said unto him, Why callest thou me good? *there is* none good but one, *that is*, God: but if thou wilt enter into life, keep the commandments.

18 He saith unto him, Which? Jesus said, Thou shalt do no murder, Thou shalt not commit adultery, Thou shalt not steal, Thou shalt not bear false witness,

19 Honour thy father and *thy* mother: and, Thou shalt love thy neighbour as thyself.

十二因為有生來是閹的、有被人閹割的、有因為天國自己不娶的。這話誰能聽、誰就可以聽。〇那時候、有人帶著孩童來見耶穌、求耶穌按手在他們頭上、為他們禱告、門徒攔阻他們。耶穌說容小孩子到我這裏來、不要禁止他們、因為在天國的、正是像小孩子這樣的人。耶穌就按手在他們頭上、離開那地方去了。〇有一個少年人進前來對耶穌說、夫子、我當行甚麼善事、纔能得永生、耶穌說你為甚麼稱我是良善的、除了　神沒有一個良善的、你要進入永生、就當謹守誡命、耶穌說就是不可殺人、不可姦淫、不可偷盜、不可妄作見證、孝敬父母、愛人如己。

ST. MATTHEW.

20 The young man saith unto him, All these things have I kept from my youth up: what lack I yet?

21 Jesus said unto him, If thou wilt be perfect, go *and* sell that thou hast, and give to the poor, and thou shalt have treasure in heaven: and come *and* follow me.

22 But when the young man heard that saying, he went away sorrowful: for he had great possessions.

23 ¶ Then said Jesus unto his disciples, Verily I say unto you, That a rich man shall hardly enter into the kingdom of heaven.

24 And again I say unto you, It is easier for a camel to go through the eye of a needle, than for a rich man to enter into the kingdom of God.

25 When his disciples heard *it*, they were exceedingly amazed, saying, Who then can be saved?

26 But Jesus beheld *them*, and said unto them, With men this is impossible; but with God all things are possible.

27 ¶ Then answered Peter and said unto him, Behold, we have forsaken all, and followed thee; what shall we have therefore?

那少年人說這些誡命我自㓗都遵守了、還有甚麼缺欠麼。耶穌說你要作完全人、去將你所有的都賣了、賙濟貧人、就必有財寶在天上、你還要來跟從我、少年人聽了這話就憂愁愁的去了、因爲他的產業甚多。○於是耶穌對門徒說我實在告訴你們、財主是難進天國的、我又告訴你們、駱駝穿過鍼的眼、比財主進　神的國還容易呢。門徒聽見甚詫異說這樣誰能得救呢。耶穌看著他們說、在人固然不能、在　神是沒有不能的。○彼得說我們捨棄一切所有的跟從你、將來能得著甚麼。

78 ST. MATTHEW.

28 And Jesus said unto them, Verily I say unto you, That ye which have followed me, in the regeneration when the Son of man shall sit in the throne of his glory, ye also shall sit upon twelve thrones, judging the twelve tribes of Israel.

29 And every one that hath forsaken houses, or brethren, or sisters, or father, or mother, or wife, or children, or lands, for my name's sake, shall receive a hundredfold, and shall inherit everlasting life.

30 But many *that are* first shall be last; and the last *shall be* first.

CHAPTER 20.

FOR the kingdom of heaven is like unto a man *that is* a householder, which went out early in the morning to hire labourers into his vineyard.

2 And when he had agreed with the labourers for a penny a day, he sent them into his vineyard.

3 And he went out about the third hour, and saw others standing idle in the market-place,

4 And said unto them; Go ye also into the vineyard, and whatsoever is right I will give you. And they went their way.

ST. MATTHEW.

5 Again he went out about the sixth and ninth hour, and did likewise.

6 And about the eleventh hour he went out, and found others standing idle, and saith unto them, Why stand ye here all the day idle?

7 They say unto him, Because no man hath hired us. He saith unto them, Go ye also into the vineyard: and whatsoever is right, *that* shall ye receive.

8 So when even was come, the lord of the vineyard saith unto his steward, Call the labourers, and give them *their* hire, beginning from the last unto the first.

9 And when they came that *were hired* about the eleventh hour, they received every man a penny.

10 But when the first came, they supposed that they should have received more; and they likewise received every man a penny.

11 And when they had received *it*, they murmured against the goodman of the house,

12 Saying, These last have wrought *but* one hour, and thou hast made them equal unto us, which have borne the burden and heat of the day.

13 But he answered one of them, and said, Friend, I do thee no wrong: didst not thou agree with me for a penny?

馬太第二十章

⁵晌午和申初時分出去也是這樣行作、酉初出去、看見又有閒站的人、就問他們說、⁶你們爲甚麼終日在這裏閒站、他們說你們也到葡萄園去所應當給的、你們必得著、⁷到了晚上園主人對管家說叫衆工人來、都給他們工錢、從後來的起、到先來的爲止酉初雇的人來了、各得一錢。⁸以爲自己必要多得誰知也是各得一錢。⁹向家主發怨言說、我們終日負苦受熱、那後來的只作了半個時辰的工夫你竟叫他們和我們一樣麼。⁺⁺主人對他們中間的一個人說朋友我不虧負你、我與你講定的工價、不是一錢麼。

ST. MATTHEW.

14 Take *that* thine *is*, and go thy way: I will give unto this last, even as unto thee.

15 Is it not lawful for me to do what I will with mine own? Is thine eye evil, because I am good?

16 So the last shall be first, and the first last: for many be called, but few chosen.

17 ¶ And Jesus going up to Jerusalem took the twelve disciples apart in the way, and said unto them,

18 Behold, we go up to Jerusalem; and the Son of man shall be betrayed unto the chief priests and unto the scribes, and they shall condemn him to death,

19 And shall deliver him to the Gentiles to mock, and to scourge, and to crucify *him:* and the third day he shall rise again.

20 ¶ Then came to him the mother of Zebedee's children with her sons, worshipping *him,* and desiring a certain thing of him.

21 And he said unto her, What wilt thou? She saith unto him, Grant that these my two sons may sit, the one on thy right hand, and the other on the left, in thy kingdom.

十章

○那時候西比太的兒子的母親帶著他兩個兒子、上前來拜耶穌、要求一件事。耶穌說你要甚麽、他說在你國裏許我這兩個兒子、一個坐在你左邊、一個坐在你右邊。

St. MATTHEW.

22 But Jesus answered and said, Ye know not what ye ask. Are ye able to drink of the cup that I shall drink of, and to be baptized with the baptism that I am baptized with? They say unto him, We are able.

23 And he saith unto them, Ye shall drink indeed of my cup, and be baptized with the baptism that I am baptized with: but to sit on my right hand, and on my left, is not mine to give, but *it shall be given to them* for whom it is prepared of my Father.

24 And when the ten heard *it*, they were moved with indignation against the two brethren.

25 But Jesus called them *unto him*, and said, Ye know that the princes of the Gentiles exercise dominion over them, and they that are great exercise authority upon them.

26 But it shall not be so among you: but whosoever will be great among you, let him be your minister;

27 And whosoever will be chief among you, let him be your servant:

28 Even as the Son of man came not to be ministered unto, but to minister, and to give his life a ransom for many.

29 And as they departed from Jericho, a great multitude followed him.

馬太第二十章

耶穌說、你們所求的、你們不知道我將喝的那一杯、你們能喝麼、我所受的洗、你們能受麼、他們說、我們能、耶穌說、我所喝的那一杯、你們也必要喝、我所受的洗、你們也必要受、只是坐在我的左右不是我可以賜的、我父爲誰豫備我*或作無我字*就賜與誰、那十個門徒聽見、就惱怒他們弟兄二人、耶穌叫了門徒來說、外邦人有君王管束他們、有大臣轄制他們、這是你們知道的、只是你們不可如此、你們中間誰要爲大、就當服事你們、誰要居首位、就當作你們的僕人、正如人子來、不是要受人的服事、乃是要服事人、並且要捨掉性命替衆人贖罪。○出耶利哥的時候許多人跟隨他、

82 ST. MATTHEW.

30 ¶ And, behold, two blind men sitting by the way side, when they heard that Jesus passed by, cried out, saying Have mercy on us, O Lord, *thou* Son of David.

31 And the multitude rebuked them, because they should hold their peace: but they cried the more, saying, Have mercy on us, O Lord, *thou* Son of David.

32 And Jesus stood still, and called them, and said, What will ye that I shall do unto you?

33 They say unto him, Lord, that our eyes may be opened.

34 So Jesus had compassion *on them*, and touched their eyes: and immediately their eyes received sight, and they followed him.

CHAPTER 21.

AND when they drew nigh unto Jerusalem, and were come to Bethphage, unto the mount of Olives, then sent Jesus two disciples,

2 Saying unto them, Go into the village over against you, and straightway ye shall find an ass tied, and a colt with her: loose *them*, and bring *them* unto me.

3 And if any *man* say aught unto you, ye shall say, The Lord hath need of them; and straightway he will send them.

馬太第二十一章

有兩個瞎子坐在道旁、聽見耶穌經過、就大聲呼叫說主大衛的子孫憐恤我們。
人責備他們、叫他們不要喧嚷、他們越發呼叫說主大衛的子孫憐恤我們耶穌站住叫他們來、對他們說要我爲你們作甚麼瞎子說主我們要眼睛能看見耶穌憐恤他們、將他們的眼睛一摸眼睛就看見了。他們從此跟從了耶穌

第二十一章

耶穌和門徒將近耶路撒冷、先到了靠橄欖山的伯法其、耶穌就差遣兩個門徒、說你們往對面村子去必要看見那裏拴著一匹驢還有一個驢駒你們解開牽到我這裏來、倘或有人問你們、就說主要用他必叫你們牽來。

ST. MATTHEW.

4 All this was done, that it might be fulfilled which was spoken by the prophet, saying,

5 Tell ye the daughter of Sion, Behold, thy King cometh unto thee, meek, and sitting upon an ass, and a colt the foal of an ass.

6 And the disciples went, and did as Jesus commanded them,

7 And brought the ass, and the colt, and put on them their clothes, and they set *him* thereon.

8 And a very great multitude spread their garments in the way; others cut down branches from the trees, and strewed *them* in the way.

9 And the multitudes that went before, and that followed, cried, saying, Hosanna to the Son of David: Blessed *is* he that cometh in the name of the Lord; Hosanna in the highest.

10 And when he was come into Jerusalem, all the city was moved, saying, Who is this?

11 And the multitude said, This is Jesus the prophet of Nazareth of Galilee.

12 ¶ And Jesus went into the temple of God, and cast out all them that sold and bought in the temple, and overthrew the tables of the money changers, and the seats of them that sold doves,

馬太第二十一章

這事正應了先知所說的話、說應當告訴郇氏說你的王到你裏去、和和平平的騎著驢後面跟隨一個驢駒門徒遵著耶穌所咐吩的去行牽了驢和驢駒來將自己的衣服搭在上面、扶著耶穌騎上眾人有將衣服鋪在道路上的、並且前前後後的眾人都大聲說大衛的子孫和散那、即求救之意奉主名來的、是應當稱頌的、在至上之處、當稱和散那。○耶穌進了耶路撒冷合城的人、都驚動了、說這是誰、眾人說這是加利利拏撒勒的先知耶穌。耶穌進了神的殿宇、將裏面作買賣的人、都趕出去、推倒兌換銀錢的人的棹子、和賣鴿子的人的凳子、

13 And said unto them, It is written, My house shall be called the house of prayer; but ye have made it a den of thieves.

14 And the blind and the lame came to him in the temple; and he healed them.

15 And when the chief priests and scribes saw the wonderful things that he did, and the children crying in the temple, and saying, Hosanna to the Son of David; they were sore displeased,

16 And said unto him, Hearest thou what these say? And Jesus saith unto them, Yea; have ye never read, Out of the mouth of babes and sucklings thou hast perfected praise?

17 ¶ And he left them, and went out of the city into Bethany; and he lodged there.

18 Now in the morning, as he returned into the city, he hungered.

19 And when he saw a fig tree in the way, he came to it, and found nothing thereon, but leaves only, and said unto it, Let no fruit grow on thee henceforward for ever And presently the fig tree withered away.

20 And when the disciples saw *it*, they marvelled, saying, How soon is the fig tree withered away!

ST. MATTHEW.

21 Jesus answered and said unto them, Verily I say unto you, If ye have faith, and doubt not, ye shall not only do this *which is done* to the fig tree, but also if ye shall say unto this mountain, Be thou removed, and be thou cast into the sea; it shall be done.

22 And all things, whatsoever ye shall ask in prayer, believing, ye shall receive.

23 ¶ And when he was come into the temple, the chief priests and the elders of the people came unto him as he was teaching, and said, By what authority doest thou these things? and who gave thee this authority?

24 And Jesus answered and said unto them, I also will ask you one thing, which if ye tell me, I in likewise will tell you by what authority I do these things.

25 The baptism of John, whence was it? from heaven, or of men? And they reasoned with themselves, saying, If we shall say, From heaven; he will say unto us, Why did ye not then believe him?

26 But if we shall say, Of men; we fear the people; for all hold John as a prophet.

耶穌說、我實在告訴你們、若是你們有信心、不疑惑、不但能作像無花果樹上這樣的事、就是吩咐這座山離開此處、投在海裏、也必成就。你們禱告的時候、若有信心、無論求甚麽必全得著。耶穌上聖殿敎訓人、祭司長和民間的長老來問耶穌說、你用甚麼權柄作這些事、賜你這權柄的是誰。耶穌回答說、我也有一句話問你們、你們若是告訴我、我就告訴你們我用甚麼權柄作這些事。約翰的洗禮是從那裏來的、是從天上來的、還是從人間來的、他們私下商議說、我們若說從天上來的、他必問我們說、你們爲何不信他、若說從人間來、我們又懼怕百姓、因爲百姓都以約翰爲先知。

27 And they answered Jesus, and said, We cannot tell. And he said unto them, Neither tell I you by what authority I do these things.

28 ¶ But what think ye? A *certain* man had two sons; and he came to the first, and said, Son, go work to day in my vineyard.

29 He answered and said, I will not; but afterward he repented, and went.

30 And he came to the second, and said likewise. And he answered and said, I *go*, sir; and went not.

31 Whether of them twain did the will of *his* father? They say unto him, The first. Jesus saith unto them, Verily I say unto you, That the publicans and the harlots go into the kingdom of God before you.

32 For John came unto you in the way of righteousness, and ye believed him not; but the publicans and the harlots believed him: and ye, when ye had seen *it*, repented not afterward, that ye might believe him.

33 ¶ Hear another parable: There was a certain householder, which planted a vineyard, and hedged it round about, and digged a winepress in it, and built a tower, and let it out to husbandmen, and went into a far county;

ST. MATTHEW.

34 And when the time of the fruit drew near, he sent his servants to the husbandmen, that they might receive the fruits of it.

35 And the husbandmen took his servants, and beat one, and killed another, and stoned another.

36 Again he sent other servants more than the first: and they did unto them likewise.

37 But last of all he sent unto them his son, saying, They will reverence my son.

38 But when the husbandmen saw the son, they said among themselves, This is the heir; come, let us kill him, and let us seize on his inheritance.

39 And they caught him, and cast *him* out of the vineyard, and slew *him*.

40 When the lord therefore of the vineyard cometh, what will he do unto those husbandmen?

41 They say unto him, He will miserably destroy those wicked men, and will let out *his* vineyard unto other husbandmen, which shall render him the fruits in their seasons.

42 Jesus saith unto them, Did ye never read in the Scriptures, The stone which the builders rejected, the same is become the head of the corner: this is the Lord's doing, and it is marvellous in our eyes?

馬太第二十一章

三四結果子的時候近了、打發他的僕人、往農夫那裏去收果子、農夫拏住他的僕人、打了一個、殺了一個、用石頭砍死一個、三六主人又打發別的僕人去、比先前還多、農夫還是那樣待他們、三七後又打發他兒子去、以為他們必要尊敬我的兒子了、農夫看見他兒子就彼此商議說、這是承接產業的、我們不如殺了他、得他的產業、三九農夫拏住他、推出葡萄園去、殺了、四十葡萄園的主人到了、將怎樣處治這農夫呢、他們回答說、他必要滅了這惡人、將葡萄園另租給能按時交果子的農夫、四二耶穌對他們說、經上說、工匠所棄的石頭作了房角的頭塊石頭、這是主所成全的事、在我們眼中甚覺希奇、這經你們沒有讀過麼。

88 ST. MATTHEW.

43 Therefore say I unto you, The kingdom of God shall be taken from you, and given to a nation bringing forth the fruits thereof.

44 And whosoever shall fall on this stone shall be broken: but on whomsoever it shall fall, it will grind him to powder.

45 And when the chief priests and Pharisees had heard his parables, they perceived that he spake of them.

46 But when they sought to lay hands on him, they feared the multitude, because they took him for a prophet.

CHAPTER 22.

AND Jesus answered and spake unto them again by parables, and said,

2 The kingdom of heaven is like unto a certain king, which made a marriage for his son,

3 And sent forth his servants to call them that were bidden to the wedding: and they would not come.

4 Again, he sent forth other servants, saying, Tell them which are bidden, Behold, I have prepared my dinner: my oxen and *my* fatlings *are* killed, and all things *are* ready: come unto the marriage.

馬太第二十二章

我所以告訴你們、神的國必從你們這裏奪去、賜給能結果子的百姓。凡落在這石頭上的、身體必碎、這石頭落在誰的身上、誰就被石頭砸爛祭司長和法利賽人聽見他的比喻、就知道他是指著他們自己說的、要捉拏他、却懼怕衆人因爲衆人以耶穌爲先知。

第二十二章

耶穌又用比喻的話對衆人說、天國如同一個王、爲他的兒子設擺娶親的筵席、打發僕人去叫那被召的人來赴席、人都不肯來、又打發別的僕人說、你們告訴那被召的人說、酒席已經豫備、我的牛和肥畜已經宰殺各樣齊全、你們就來赴席、

5 But they made light of *it*, and went their ways, one to his farm, another to his merchandise:

6 And the remnant took his servants, and entreated *them* spitefully, and slew *them*.

7 But when the king heard *thereof*, he was wroth: and he sent forth his armies, and destroyed those murderers, and burned up their city.

8 Then saith he to his servants, The wedding is ready, but they which were bidden were not worthy.

9 Go ye therefore into the highways, and as many as ye shall find, bid to the marriage.

10 So those servants went out into the highways, and gathered together all as many as they found, both bad and good: and the wedding was furnished with guests.

11 ¶ And when the king came in to see the guests, he saw there a man which had not on a wedding garment:

12 And he saith unto him, Friend, how camest thou in hither not having a wedding garment? And he was speechless.

13 Then said the king to the servants, Bind him hand and foot, and take him away, and cast *him* into outer darkness; there shall be weeping and gnashing of teeth.

14 For many are called, but few *are* chosen.

那些人不理就走了、一個到自己田裏去、一個上市去、其餘的人拏住僕人、凌辱他將他殺了。王聽見大怒發兵滅了那兇手將他們一城都燒毀了。就對僕人說筵席已經豫備好了只是所召的人不配、現在你們可往通行的大路上去無論遇見誰、都叫來赴席僕人出去到了路上凡所遇見的人不論善惡都領了來、坐滿了筵席。王進來觀看坐席的人見那裏有一個沒有穿禮服的、就對他說朋友你到這裏來為甚麼不穿禮服。那人無話回答王就吩咐僕人說捆綁這人的手足、將他丟在外面黑暗地方去在那裏必要哀哭切齒了。因為被召的人多選上的人少。

15 ¶ Then went the Pharisees, and took counsel how they might entangle him in *his* talk. 16 And they sent out unto him their disciples with the Herodians, saying, Master, we know that thou art true, and teachest the way of God in truth, neither carest thou for any *man:* for thou regardest not the person of men. 17 Tell us therefore, What thinkest thou? Is it lawful to give tribute unto Cesar, or not? 18 But Jesus perceived their wickedness, and said, Why tempt ye me, *ye* hypocrites? 19 Shew me the tribute money. And they brought unto him a penny. 20 And he saith unto them, Whose *is* this image and superscription? 21 They say unto him, Cesar's. Then saith he unto them, Render therefore unto Cesar the things which are Cesar's; and unto God the things that are God's. 22 When they had heard *these words,* they marvelled, and left him, and went their way. 23 ¶ The same day came to him the Sadducees, which say that there is no resurrection, and asked him,	〇那時候法利賽人出去、大家商量、要就著耶穌所說的話陷害他。就打發徒弟和希律一黨的人去見耶穌說夫子、我們知道你是誠寶人也誠誠實實的傳 神的道待人、是不狥情的、取人是不論相貌的、請告訴我們納稅給該撒、你以為應當不應當耶穌知道他們的惡意就說假冒為善的人為甚麼試探我、拏一個上稅的銀錢來給我看。他們就拏了一個銀錢來給耶穌、耶穌對他們說這像和這號是誰的。他們說、是該撒的耶穌說這樣該撒的東西當歸給該撒、 神的東西當歸給 神、他們聽見甚以為希奇就離開耶穌去了。〇撒都該人常說人死不能復活那時候他們有幾個人來見耶穌說、

24 Saying, Master, Moses said, If a man die, having no children, his brother shall marry his wife, and raise up seed unto his brother.

25 Now there were with us seven brethren: and the first, when he had married a wife, deceased, and, having no issue, left his wife unto his brother:

26 Likewise the second also, and the third, unto the seventh.

27 And last of all the woman died also.

28 Therefore in the resurrection, whose wife shall she be of the seven? for they all had her.

29 Jesus answered and said unto them, Ye do err, not knowing the Scriptures, nor the power of God.

30 For in the resurrection they neither marry, nor are given in marriage, but are as the angels of God in heaven.

31 But as touching the resurrection of the dead, have ye not read that which was spoken unto you by God, saying,

32 I am the God of Abraham, and the God of Isaac, and the God of Jacob? God is not the God of the dead, but of the living.

33 And when the multitude heard *this*, they were astonished at his doctrine.

34 ¶ But when the Pharisees had heard that he had put the Sadducees to silence, they were gathered together.

二四夫子、摩西說人若死了沒有兒子、他兄弟就當娶他的妻子生兒子承繼哥哥我們
二五那裏有弟兄七人、居長的娶了妻子死了沒有兒子留下妻子給他兄弟、第二第三
二六直到第七、都是這樣後來婦人也死了、
二七那七個人中間誰的妻子呢。耶穌回答說你們錯了、你們不明白聖經、也不曉
二八算是那七個人既是都娶過他到復活的時候、他
得 神的大能復活之後人都不娶不嫁、如 神的使者在天上一樣。論到人死復
活 經上有 神曉諭你們的話你們沒有讀過麼、 神說我是亞伯拉罕的 神、以
撒的 神雅各的 神、 神不是死人的 神乃是活人的 神衆人聽見耶穌的
教訓、甚是詫異。○法利賽人聽見耶穌塞住撒都該人的口、就在那裏聚集

35 Then one of them, *which was* a lawyer, asked *him a question*, tempting him, and saying,

36 Master, which *is* the great commandment in the law?

37 Jesus said unto him, Thou shalt love the Lord thy God with all thy heart, and with all thy soul, and with all thy mind.

38 This is the first and great commandment.

39 And the second *is* like unto it, Thou shalt love thy neighbour as thyself.

40 On these two commandments hang all the law and the prophets.

41 ¶ While the Pharisees were gathered together, Jesus asked them,

42 Saying, What think ye of Christ? whose son is he? They say unto him, *The son* of David.

43 He saith unto them, How then doth David in spirit call him Lord, saying,

44 The LORD said unto my Lord, Sit thou on my right hand, till I make thine enemies thy footstool?

45 If David then call him Lord, how is he his son?

46 And no man was able to answer him a word, neither durst any *man* from that day forth ask him any more *questions*.

三五、他們中間有一個教法師、試探耶穌說、夫子、律法上所載的誡命那一條是最大的。
三六、耶穌說、你常盡心盡性盡意愛主你的　神、這是頭一條最大的誡其次愛人如己、
三七、也是這樣。這兩條誠是律法和先知一切道理的總綱。○
四一、法利賽人聚集的時候、耶穌問他們說、論到基督你們以為怎樣他是誰的後裔呢、他們回答說、是大衛的後裔。
耶穌說這樣、大衛被聖靈感助、怎麼又稱基督為主說、主對我的主說、坐在我的右邊、等我使你的仇敵為你的腳凳。大衛既稱基督為主基督如何是大衛的後裔呢。
衆人都無言可答從此沒有人敢再問他了。

ST. MATTHEW.

CHAPTER 23.

THEN spake Jesus to the multitude, and to his disciples,

2 Saying, The scribes and the Pharisees sit in Moses' seat:

3 All therefore whatsoever they bid you observe, *that* observe and do; but do not ye after their works: for they say, and do not.

4 For they bind heavy burdens and grievous to be borne, and lay *them* on men's shoulders; but they *themselves* will not move them with one of their fingers.

5 But all their works they do for to be seen of men: they make broad their phylacteries, and enlarge the borders of their garments,

6 And love the uppermost rooms at feasts, and the chief seats in the synagogues,

7 And greetings in the markets, and to be called of men, Rabbi, Rabbi.

8 But be not ye called Rabbi: for one is your Master, *even* Christ; and all ye are brethren.

9 And call no *man* your father upon the earth: for one is your Father, which is in heaven.

94 St. MATTHEW.

10 Neither be ye called masters: for one is your Master, *even* Christ.

11 But he that is greatest among you shall be your servant.

12 And whosoever shall exalt himself shall be abased; and he that shall humble himself shall be exalted.

13 ¶ But woe unto you, scribes and Pharisees, hypocrites! for ye shut up the kingdom of heaven against men: for ye neither go in *yourselves*, neither suffer ye them that are entering to go in.

14 Woe unto you scribes and Pharisees, hypocrites! for ye devour widows' houses, and for a pretence make long prayer: therefore ye shall receive the greater damnation.

15 Woe unto you, scribes and Pharisees, hypocrites! for ye compass sea and land to make one proselyte; and when he is made, ye make him twofold more the child of hell than yourselves.

16 Woe unto you, *ye* blind guides, which say, Whosoever shall swear by the temple, it is nothing; but whosoever shall swear by the gold of the temple, he is a debtor!

馬太第二十三章

也不可受師尊的稱呼、你們只有一位師尊、就是基督、你們中間誰要為大、誰就應當作你們的僕人、因為自高的必降卑了、自卑的必升高了、○你們這些假冒為善的讀書人法利賽人、是必有禍的、因為你們在人面前關了天國的門、自己不進去、有人要進去你們也不容他進去、○你們這些假冒為善的讀書人法利賽人、是必有禍的、因為你們侵吞了寡婦的家財、假意作常常的祈禱、所以你們受罰必更重了、○你們這些假冒為善的讀書人法利賽人、是必有禍的、因為你們走遍千山萬水、引一個人入教、入了教、却叫他作地獄裏的人、比你們還加倍的、○你們這些瞎眼領人的、是必有禍的、你們說指著殿起誓、是不要緊的、指著殿裏的金子起誓、就當謹守、

ST. MATTHEW.

17 *Ye* fools and blind: for whether is greater, the gold, or the temple that sanctifieth the gold?

18 And, Whosoever shall swear by the altar, it is nothing; but whosoever sweareth by the gift that is upon it, he is guilty.

19 *Ye* fools and blind: for whether *is* greater, the gift, or the altar that sanctifieth the gift?

20 Whoso therefore shall swear by the altar, sweareth by it, and by all things thereon.

21 And whoso shall swear by the temple, sweareth by it, and by him that dwelleth therein.

22 And he that shall swear by heaven, sweareth by the throne of God, and by him that sitteth thereon.

23 Woe unto you, scribes and Pharisees, hypocrites! for ye pay tithe of mint and anise and cummin, and have omitted the weightier *matters* of the law, judgment, mercy, and faith: these ought ye to have done, and not to leave the other undone.

24 *Ye* blind guides, which strain at a gnat, and swallow a camel.

叉糊塗叉瞎眼的人、甚麼是大的、是金子大、還是叫金子成爲聖物的殿大。
你們叉說、指著壇起誓、是不要緊的、指著壇上的供物起誓、就當謹守叉糊塗叉眼瞎的人、甚麼是大的、是供物大還是叫供物成爲聖物的壇大。人若指著壇起誓、就是指著壇和壇上的一切東西起誓。人指著殿起誓、就是指著殿和住在殿裏的起誓。人指著天起誓、就是指著神的寶座和坐在上面的起誓。你們這些假冒爲善的讀書人法利賽人、是必有禍的。因爲你們將薄荷茴香芹菜十分之一獻上、反將律法中最要緊的道理就是公義仁愛誠實丟棄了、這是應當行的、那也是不可丟棄的瞎眼領人的、蚊子你們就濾出來、駱駝你們倒吞下去。

ST. MATTHEW.

25 Woe unto you, scribes and Pharisees, hypocrites! for ye make clean the outside of the cup and of the platter, but within they are full of extortion and excess.

26 *Thou* blind Pharisee, cleanse first that *which is* within the cup and platter, that the outside of them may be clean also.

27 Woe unto you, scribes and Pharisees, hypocrites! for ye are like unto whited sepulchres, which indeed appear beautiful outward, but are within full of dead *men's* bones, and of all uncleanness.

28 Even so ye also outwardly appear righteous unto men, but within ye are full of hypocrisy and iniquity.

29 Woe unto you, scribes and Pharisees, hypocrites! because ye build the tombs of the prophets, and garnish the sepulchres of the righteous,

30 And say, If we had been in the days of our fathers, we would not have been partakers with them in the blood of the prophets.

31 Wherefore ye be witnesses unto yourselves, that ye are the children of them which killed the prophets.

32 Fill ye up then the measure of your fathers.

馬太第二十三章

你們這些假冒爲善的讀書人法利賽人、是必有禍的因爲你們洗淨杯盤的外面、裏面却盛滿了搶奪和不義的物瞎眼的法利賽人先潔淨了杯盤的裏面那外面自然也潔淨了。你們這些假冒爲善的讀書人法利賽人、是必有禍的因爲你們如同修飾的墳墓原文作抹灰的墳墓外面好看裏面却是死人的骨頭和各樣污穢的物。這樣你們外面在人前似乎是善裏面却裝滿了假善和不法的事。你們這些假冒爲善的讀書人法利賽人、是必有禍的因爲你們建造先知的墳修飾義人的墓又說、若是我們在我們祖宗的時候、必不和他們同謀殺害先知這就是你們自己見證你們是殺害先知的人的後代了你們去滿盈你們祖宗的惡貫罷。

ST. MATTHEW.

33 *Ye* serpents, *ye* generation of vipers, how can ye escape the damnation of hell?

34 ¶ Wherefore, behold, I send unto you prophets, and wise men, and scribes: and *some* of them ye shall kill and crucify; and *some* of them shall ye scourge in your synagogues, and persecute *them* from city to city:

35 That upon you may come all the righteous blood shed upon the earth, from the blood of righteous Abel unto the blood of Zacharias son of Barachias, whom ye slew between the temple and the altar.

36 Verily I say unto you, All these things shall come upon this generation.

37 O Jerusalem, Jerusalem, *thou* that killest the prophets, and stonest them which are sent unto thee, how often would I have gathered thy children together, even as a hen gathereth her chickens under *her* wings, and ye would not!

38 Behold, your house is left unto you desolate.

毒蛇一類的人、你們怎能逃脫地獄的刑罰呢。我差遣先知和賢人並讀書人、到你們那裏去、這些人將來有被你們殺害的、有被你們釘十字架的、有被你們在會堂鞭打的、有被你們從這城追逼到那城的、這樣、凡世上殺害義人的罪、都要歸在你們身上、就是從殺害義人亞伯起、直到你們在殿壇中間殺害巴拉加的兒子撒加利亞為止。我實在告訴你們、這些罪都要歸在這世代了耶路撒冷阿、耶路撒冷阿、你常殺害先知又用石頭砍死那奉差遣到你這裏來的人、我多次要聚集你的子民、如同母雞將小雞聚集在翅膀底下一般、只是你不願意。你的家將要變為荒場。

98 ST. MATTHEW.

39 For I say unto you, Ye shall not see me henceforth, till ye shall say, Blessed *is* he that cometh in the name of the Lord.

CHAPTER 24.

AND Jesus went out, and departed from the temple: and his disciples came to *him* for to shew him the buildings of the temple.

2 And Jesus said unto them, See ye not all these things? verily I say unto you, There shall not be left here one stone upon another, that shall not be thrown down.

3 ¶ And as he sat upon the mount of Olives, the disciples came unto him privately, saying, Tell us, when shall these things be? and what *shall be* the sign of thy coming, and of the end of the world?

4 And Jesus answered and said unto them, Take heed that no man deceive you.

5 For many shall come in my name, saying, I am Christ; and shall deceive many.

第二十四章

一耶穌出了聖殿門徒進前請他觀看殿宇耶穌對他們說你們看見這殿宇麼我實在告訴你們、在這裏將來沒有一塊石頭留在石頭上都必被拆毀了耶穌在橄欖山上坐著門徒暗暗的上前來說請告訴我們甚麼時候有這事你降臨和世界的末日有甚麼豫兆耶穌說你們須要小心恐怕被人迷惑了因爲將來有許多冒我名來的、自稱是基督要迷惑許多人

我告訴你們、從今以後你們不能再見我、必要等到你們說奉主名來的是有福的那時候了。

ST. MATTHEW.

6 And ye shall hear of wars and rumours of wars: see that ye be not troubled: for all *these things* must come to pass, but the end is not yet.

7 For nation shall rise against nation, and kingdom against kingdom: and there shall be famines, and pestilences, and earthquakes, in divers places.

8 All these *are* the beginning of sorrows.

9 Then shall they deliver you up to be afflicted, and shall kill you: and ye shall be hated of all nations for my name's sake.

10 And then shall many be offended, and shall betray one another, and shall hate one another.

11 And many false prophets shall rise, and shall deceive many.

12 And because iniquity shall abound, the love of many shall wax cold.

13 But he that shall endure unto the end, the same shall be saved.

14 And this gospel of the kingdom shall be preached in all the world for a witness unto all nations; and then shall the end come.

15 When ye therefore shall see the abomination of desolation, spoken of by Daniel the prophet, stand in the holy place, (whoso readeth, let him understand;)

你們將來聽見打仗、和打仗的風聲、不要懼怕、這事是必有的、只是末日還沒有到。民要攻擊民國要攻擊國饑荒瘟疫地震各處都有、這都是災難的起頭。那時候、人要將你們陷在患難裏、要為殺你們、並且你們要為我的名、被萬國人怨恨。那時候、必有許多人厭棄我的道、彼此互相陷害、互相怨恨。許多假先知起來、迷惑許多人。因為罪惡眾多許多人的愛心漸漸冷淡了。惟有忍耐到底的、必要得救。天國的福音、將要傳遍普天下、與萬民作見證、然後末日臨到你們看見先知但以理所說殘暴可憎的物站在聖地讀這經的人應當思想。

ST. MATTHEW.

16 Then let them which be in Judea flee into the mountains:

17 Let him which is on the house-top not come down to take any thing out of his house:

18 Neither let him which is in the field return back to take his clothes.

19 And woe unto them that are with child, and to them that give suck in those days!

20 But pray ye that your flight be not in the winter, neither on the sabbath day:

21 For then shall be great tribulation, such as was not since the beginning of the world to this time, no, nor ever shall be.

22 And except those days should be shortened, there should no flesh be saved: but for the elect's sake those days shall be shortened.

23 Then if any man shall say unto you, Lo, here is Christ, or there; believe *it* not.

24 For there shall arise false Christs, and false prophets, and shall shew great signs and wonders; insomuch that, if *it were* possible, they shall deceive the very elect.

25 Behold, I have told you before.

26 Wherefore if they shall say unto you, Behold, he is in the desert; go not forth: behold, *he is* in the secret chambers; believe *it* not.

馬太第二十四章

那時候、住在猶太國的、應當逃到山上、在房上的、不要下來取家裏的東西、在田裏的、不要囘來取衣服。那時候、懷孕的和乳養嬰孩的婦人有禍了。你們應當祈禱免得你們逃走的時候、遇見冬天和安息日。那時候、必有大災難從創世以來直到今沒有這樣的災難後來也是不能有的。若不減少那日子、就沒有一個人得救只是爲那揀選的人那日子必要減少了。那時候、若有人告訴你說、基督在這裏、基督在那裏、不可信他。因爲假基督假先知將要起來、施行大異蹟大奇事、若能迷惑揀選的人也就迷惑了。這事我都像先告訴你們了。若有人對你們說、基督在曠野裏、你們不可出去說基督在嚴密的屋子裏、你們不可信他。

ST. MATTHEW.

27 For as the lightning cometh out of the east, and shineth even unto the west; so shall also the coming of the Son of man be.

28 For wheresoever the carcass is, there will the eagles be gathered together.

29 ¶ Immediately after the tribulation of those days shall the sun be darkened, and the moon shall not give her light, and the stars shall fall from heaven, and the powers of the heavens shall be shaken:

30 And then shall appear the sign of the Son of man in heaven: and then shall all the tribes of the earth mourn, and they shall see the Son of man coming in the clouds of heaven with power and great glory.

31 And he shall send his angels with a great sound of a trumpet, and they shall gather together his elect from the four winds, from one end of heaven to the other.

32 Now learn a parable of the fig tree; When his branch is yet tender, and putteth forth leaves, ye know that summer is nigh:

33 So likewise ye, when ye shall see all these things, know that it is near, *even* at the doors.

34 Verily I say unto you, This generation shall not pass, till all these things be fulfilled.

閃電從東邊放光、就照到西邊、人子降臨也是這樣。屍首在那裏、鷹也必聚在那裏。

這災難之後忽然日頭黑暗月不放光衆星從天上墜落天象都要震動那時人子的兆頭必現在天上地上各族的人、都要哀哭、看見人子有大權柄、大榮耀、駕著天上的雲來他必差遣他的使者吹號筒、聲音甚大將所揀選的民從天邊四極都招聚了來。○你們可以拏無花果樹作比方、當樹枝柔嫩發葉的時候、就知道夏天快到了你們看見這些兆頭也就知道那時候近了、已在門前了。我實在告訴你們這世代還沒有過去這些事必都成就。

35 Heaven and earth shall pass away, but my words shall not pass away.

36 ¶ But of that day and hour knoweth no *man*, no, not the angels of heaven, but my Father only.

37 But as the days of Noe *were*, so shall also the coming of the Son of man be.

38 For as in the days that were before the flood they were eating and drinking, marrying and giving in marriage, until the day that Noe entered into the ark,

39 And knew not until the flood came, and took them all away; so shall also the coming of the Son of man be.

40 Then shall two be in the field; the one shall be taken, and the other left.

41 Two *women shall be* grinding at the mill; the one shall be taken, and the other left.

42 ¶ Watch therefore; for ye know not what hour your Lord doth come.

43 But know this, that if the goodman of the house had known in what watch the thief would come, he would have watched, and would not have suffered his house to be broken up.

44 Therefore be ye also ready; for in such an hour as ye think not the Son of man cometh.

ST. MATTHEW.

45 Who then is a faithful and wise servant, whom his lord hath made ruler over his household, to give them meat in due season?

46 Blessed *is* that servant, whom his lord when he cometh shall find so doing.

47 Verily I say unto you, That he shall make him ruler over all his goods.

48 But and if that evil servant shall say in his heart, My lord delayeth his coming;

49 And shall begin to smite *his* fellow servants, and to eat and drink with the drunken;

50 The lord of that servant shall come in a day when he looketh not for *him*, and in an hour that he is not aware of,

51 And shall cut him asunder, and appoint *him* his portion with the hypocrites: there shall be weeping and gnashing of teeth.

CHAPTER 25.

THEN shall the kingdom of heaven be likened unto ten virgins, which took their lamps, and went forth to meet the bridegroom.

2 And five of them were wise, and five *were* foolish.

3 They that *were* foolish took their lamps, and took no oil with them:

誰是忠信聰明的僕人、家主用他管理家人、按著時候分糧呢。主人回來看見他這樣辦事、這僕人就有福了。我實在告訴你們、主必用他管理全家事務。倘若那惡僕心裏說我主人來的必遲、就打起他的同伴來、又和酒醉的人、一同吃喝在想不到的日子、不知道的時候、那僕人的主人必來重重的處治他、趕他到假冒爲善的人的地方和他們一樣受刑、在那裏必要哀哭切齒了。

第二十五章

一那時候天國比如十個童女拏燈出去迎接新郎、二五個是聰明的、五個是愚拙的。三愚拙的拏著燈、不豫備油、

104 ST. MATTHEW.

4 But the wise took oil in their vessels with their lamps.

5 While the bridegroom tarried, they all slumbered and slept.

6 And at midnight there was a cry made, Behold, the bridegroom cometh; go ye out to meet him.

· 7 Then all those virgins arose, and trimmed their lamps,

8 And the foolish said unto the wise, Give us of your oil; for our lamps are gone out.

9 But the wise answered, saying, *Not so*; lest there be not enough for us and you: but go ye rather to them that sell, and buy for yourselves.

10 And while they went to buy, the bridegroom came; and they that were ready went in with him to the marriage: and the door was shut.

11 Afterward came also the other virgins, saying, Lord, open to us.

12 But he answered and said, Verily I say unto you, I know you not.

13 Watch therefore; for ye know neither the day nor the hour wherein the Son of man cometh.

14 ¶ For *the kingdom of heaven is* as a man travelling into a far country, *who* called his own servants, and delivered unto them his goods.

馬太第二十五章

聰明的擎著燈、豫備油在器皿裏。新郎來得遲、他們都在那裏打盹睡著了半夜有人喊叫說、新郎到了、你們出去迎接衆童女都起來、整理他們的燈。愚拙的對聰明的說、我們的燈要滅了、請分給我們一點油聰明的回答說、恐怕不彀你我用的、如你自己到油坊去買正買去的時候、新郎來了、豫備油的童女同他進了筵席、門就關了後來那其餘的童女到了、說主阿、主阿、請給我們開門。回答說我實在告訴你們我不認識你們這樣你們必當儆醒、因爲不知道人子甚麼日子、甚麼時候臨到。○天國又比如一個人將要出外叫衆僕人來、將所有的家財交給他們。

ST. MATTHEW.

15 And unto one he gave five talents, to another two, and to another one ; to every man according to his several ability ; and straightway took his journey.

16 Then he that had received the five talents went and traded with the same, and made *them* other five talents.

17 And likewise he that *had received* two, he also gained other two.

18 But he that had received one went and digged in the earth, and hid his lord's money.

19 After a long time the lord of those servants cometh, and reckoneth with them.

20 And so he that had received five talents came and brought other five talents, saying, Lord, thou deliveredst unto me five talents : behold, I have gained beside them five talents more.

21 His lord said unto him, Well done, *thou* good and faithful servant : thou hast been faithful over a few things, I will make thee ruler over many things : enter thou into the joy of thy lord.

22 He also that had received two talents came and said, Lord, thou deliveredst unto me two talents : behold, I have gained two other talents beside them.

馬太第二十五章

按著他們的才幹、有給五千銀的、有給二千的、有給一千的、主人就出外去了、那領五千的拏去作買賣又賺了五千、那領二千的又賺了二千只有那領一千的、掘地將主人的銀子埋藏了過了許久主人回來與僕人算賬那領五千的、又拏著那另外的五千、進前來說主交給我五千、我又賺了五千了主人說好、你這善良忠義的僕人你在小事上既有忠心我要交給你大事管理可以進來和你主人同享安樂領二千的也來說主交給我二千、我又賺了二千。

106 ST. MATTHEW.

23 His lord said unto him, Well done, good and faithful servant; thou hast been faithful over a few things, I will make thee ruler over many things: enter thou into the joy of thy lord.

24 Then he which had received the one talent came and said, Lord, I knew thee that thou art a hard man, reaping where thou hast not sown, and gathering where thou hast not strewed:

25 And I was afraid, and went and hid thy talent in the earth: lo, *there* thou hast *that is* thine.

26 His lord answered and said unto him, *Thou* wicked and slothful servant, thou knewest that I reap where I sowed not, and gather where I have not strewed:

27 Thou oughtest therefore to have put my money to the exchangers, and *then* at my coming I should have received mine own with usury.

28 Take therefore the talent from him, and give *it* unto him which hath ten talents.

29 For unto every one that hath shall be given, and he shall have abundance: but from him that hath not shall be taken away even that which he hath.

馬太第二十五章

主人說、你這善良忠義的僕人、你在小事上既有忠心我要交給你大事管理可以進來和你主人同享安樂那領一千的來說主我知道你是忍心的人沒有種的地方要收割沒有散的地方要聚斂所以我懼怕將你的一千銀子埋藏在地裏如今將你的本還你。主人說你這懶惰的惡奴才既知道我沒有種的地方要收割沒有散的地方要聚斂就當把我的銀子放給兌換銀錢的人好叫我回來時候得本又得利可以奪過他這一千來交給那有十千的因為有的、還要給他叫他有餘沒有的、連他所有的也必奪過來。

ST. MATTHEW.

30 And cast ye the unprofitable servant into outer darkness: there shall be weeping and gnashing of teeth.

31 ¶ When the Son of man shall come in his glory, and all the holy angels with him, then shall he sit upon the throne of his glory:

32 And before him shall be gathered all nations: and he shall separate them one from another, as a shepherd divideth *his* sheep from the goats:

33 And he shall set the sheep on his right hand, but the goats on the left.

34 Then shall the King say unto them on his right hand, Come, ye blessed of my Father, inherit the kingdom prepared for you from the foundation of the world:

35 For I was a hungered, and ye gave me meat: I was thirsty, and ye gave me drink: I was a stranger, and ye took me in:

36 Naked, and ye clothed me: I was sick, and ye visited me: I was in prison, and ye came unto me.

37 Then shall the righteous answer him, saying, Lord, when saw we thee a hungered, and fed *thee?* or thirsty, and gave *thee* drink?

馬太第二十五章

將那無用的僕人、趕到外面黑暗地方去、在那裏必要哀哭切齒了。○當人子顯榮耀帶領聖天使降臨的時候、要坐在有榮耀的寶座上、萬民都聚集在他面前、必將他們分別出來、如同牧羊的分別綿羊山羊、綿羊在右邊、山羊在左邊。王要對那在右邊的說、蒙我父寵愛的、可來承受創世以來、爲你們所豫備的國、因爲我餓了你們給我吃、渴了你們給我喝、我作客旅你們留我住、我赤身露體、你們給我衣裳、穿、我病了你們看顧我、我在監裏你們來看我、衆義人要說、主我甚麽時候見你餓了給你吃、渴了給你喝、

108 ST. MATTHEW.

38 When saw we thee a stranger, and took *thee* in? or naked, and clothed *thee*?

39 Or when saw we thee sick, or in prison, and came unto thee?

40 And the King shall answer and say unto them, Verily I say unto you, Inasmuch as ye have done *it* unto one of the least of these my brethren, ye have done *it* unto me.

41 Then shall he say also unto them on the left hand, Depart from me, ye cursed, into everlasting fire, prepared for the devil and his angels:

42 For I was a hungered, and ye gave me no meat: I was thirsty, and ye gave me no drink:

43 I was a stranger, and ye took me not in: naked, and ye clothed me not; sick, and in prison, and ye visited me not.

44 Then shall they also answer him, saying, Lord, when saw we thee a hungered, or athirst, or a stranger, or naked, or sick, or in prison, and did not minister unto thee?

45 Then shall he answer them, saying, Verily I say unto you, Inasmuch as ye did *it* not to one of the least of these, ye did *it* not to me.

馬太第二十五章

甚麼時候見你作客旅留你住、赤身露體給你衣裳穿、又甚麼時候見你或是有病、或是在監裏、來看你呢。王要回答說我實在告訴你們、這事既作在我一個最小的兄弟身上、就是作在我的身上了。又對那在左邊的說你們這些可咒詛的人、離開我進入爲魔鬼和魔鬼的使者所豫備的永火裏去、因爲我餓了你們不給我吃、渴了你們不給我喝、我作客旅你們不留我住、赤身露體你們不給我衣裳穿、我有病、或是在監裏你們也要說主我甚麼時候見你或餓、或渴、或是作客旅、或是赤身露體、或是有病、或是在監裏、不服事你呢、王要回答說我實在告訴你們、這事既不作在我一個最小的兄弟身上、就是不作在我的身上了。

ST. MATTHEW.

46 And these shall go away into everlasting punishment: but the righteous into life eternal.

CHAPTER 26.

AND it came to pass, when Jesus had finished all these sayings, he said unto his disciples,

2 Ye know that after two days is *the feast of* the passover, and the Son of man is betrayed to be crucified.

3 Then assembled together the chief priests, and the scribes, and the elders of the people, unto the palace of the high priest, who was called Caiaphas,

4 And consulted that they might take Jesus by subtilty, and kill *him*.

5 But they said, Not on the feast *day*, lest there be an uproar among the people.

6 ¶ Now when Jesus was in Bethany, in the house of Simon the leper,

7 There came unto him a woman having an alabaster box of very precious ointment, and poured it on his head, as he sat at meat.

8 But when his disciples saw *it*, they had indignation, saying, To what purpose *is* this waste?

第二十六章

耶穌說完了這些話、對門徒說、你們是知道的、過兩日就是逾越節、人子將要被釘在十字架上了。那時候、眾祭司長和讀書人民間的長老聚集在大祭司該亞法的院裏、大家商議、要用詭計拏住耶穌殺他、只是他們說當節的日子不可拏他、恐怕民間生亂○耶穌在伯大尼長過癩的西門家裏坐席的時候、有一個婦人拏著玉盒裏面盛著極貴的香膏前來將膏澆在耶穌頭上門徒看見就不喜悅說何必這樣糜費、

ST. MATTHEW.

9 For this ointment might have been sold for much, and given to the poor.

10 When Jesus understood *it*, he said unto them, Why trouble ye the woman? for she hath wrought a good work upon me.

11 For ye have the poor always with you; but me ye have not always.

12 For in that she hath poured this ointment on my body, she did *it* for my burial.

13 Verily I say unto you, Wheresoever this gospel shall be preached in the whole world, *there* shall also this, that this woman hath done, be told for a memorial of her.

14 ¶ Then one of the twelve, called Judas Iscariot, went unto the chief priests,

15 And said *unto them*, What will ye give me, and I will deliver him unto you? And they covenanted with him for thirty pieces of silver.

16 And from that time he sought opportunity to betray him.

17 ¶ Now the first *day* of the *feast of* unleavened bread the disciples came to Jesus, saying unto him, Where wilt thou that we prepare for thee to eat the passover?

馬太第二十六章

這香膏可以賣許多的銀子、賙濟貧人。耶穌知道他們的意念、就說爲甚麼難爲這婦人、他向我所作的、是一件好事、貧人常和你們在一處、我不常和你們在一處。他將香膏澆在我身上、是爲我安葬作的。我實在告訴你們、普天之下、無論在何處傳福音、總要述說這婦人所行的、叫人記念他。○那時候、十二門徒裏、有一個門徒名叫以色加略猶大、去見衆祭司長、說我將他賣給你們、你們願意給我多少銀子、就講定了三十塊銀錢。從此猶大尋找機會要賣耶穌。○除酵節的頭一日、門徒進前來、問耶穌說、你吃逾越節的羔羊、要我們在何處豫備。

ST. MATTHEW.

18 And he said, Go into the city to such a man, and say unto him, The Master saith, My time is at hand; I will keep the passover at thy house with my disciples.

19 And the disciples did as Jesus had appointed them; and they made ready the passover.

20 Now when the even was come, he sat down with the twelve.

21 And as they did eat, he said, Verily I say unto you, that one of you shall betray me.

22 And they were exceeding sorrowful, and began every one of them to say unto him, Lord, is it I?

23 And he answered and said, He that dippeth *his* hand with me in the dish, the same shall betray me.

24 The Son of man goeth as it is written of him: but woe unto that man by whom the Son of man is betrayed! it had been good for that man if he had not been born.

25 Then Judas, which betrayed him, answered and said, Master, is it I? He said unto him, Thou hast said.

26 ¶ And as they were eating, Jesus took bread, and blessed *it*, and brake *it*, and gave *it* to the disciples, and said, Take, eat; this is my body.

耶穌說、你們進城去、到某人那裏、對他說、夫子說、我的時候快到了、我和門徒要在你家設擺逾越節的筵席、門徒遵著耶穌所吩咐的行、就豫備了逾越節的筵席。到了晚上耶穌和十二門徒坐席正吃的時候耶穌說我實在告訴你們、你們中間有一個人要賣我了。門徒就甚憂愁、一個一個的問耶穌說主是我麼耶穌說、和我一同蘸手在盤子裏的、他就是賣我的。人子必要照著經上所指著他說的話去世、只是賣人子的人必定有禍了、這人倒不如不生在世上、賣耶穌的猶大問耶穌說、夫子、是我麼耶穌說、你說得是了。○吃的時候、耶穌拏起餅來、祝謝了、擘開分給門徒、說你們拏這個吃這是我的身體。

ST. MATTHEW.

27 And he took the cup, and gave thanks, and gave it to them, saying, Drink ye all of it;

28 For this is my blood of the new testament, which is shed for many for the remission of sins.

29 But I say unto you, I will not drink henceforth of this fruit of the vine, until that day when I drink it new with you in my Father's kingdom.

30 And when they had sung a hymn, they went out into the mount of Olives.

31 Then saith Jesus unto them, All ye shall be offended because of me this night: for it is written, I will smite the Shepherd, and the sheep of the flock shall be scattered abroad.

32 But after I am risen again, I will go before you into Galilee.

33 Peter answered and said unto him, Though all *men* shall be offended because of thee, *yet* will I never be offended.

34 Jesus said unto him, Verily, I say unto thee, That this night, before the cock crow, thou shalt deny me thrice.

35 Peter said unto him, Though I should die with thee, yet will I not deny thee. Likewise also said all the disciples.

36 ¶ Then cometh Jesus with them unto a place called Gethsemane, and saith unto the disciples, Sit ye here, while I go and pray yonder.

又擎起杯來、祝謝了、遞給門徒、說、你們都喝這個、這是我的血、就是新約的血、爲赦衆人的罪流出來的、我告訴你們、從今日直到我和你們在我父國裏喝新酒的那日子、我不再喝這葡萄汁了、他們歌了詩、就出來往橄欖山去、那時候、耶穌對門徒說、這夜裏你們都要棄絕我、因爲經上說、我要打牧羊的、羊羣就都散了、我復活之後要在你們以先往加利利去、彼得說、衆人雖然棄絕你、我永不棄絕你、耶穌說、我實在告訴你、這夜裏雞叫以先、你要三次說不認識我、彼得說、我就是和你同死、也不說不認識你、衆門徒也都如此說、○ 耶穌和門徒到了一個地方、叫作客西馬尼、耶穌對門徒說、你們坐在這裏、我到那邊去禱告、

ST. MATTHEW.

37 And he took with him Peter and the two sons of Zebedee, and began to be sorrowful and very heavy.

38 Then saith he unto them, My soul is exceeding sorrowful, even unto death: tarry ye here, and watch with me.

39 And he went a little further, and fell on his face, and prayed, saying, O my Father, if it be possible, let this cup pass from me: nevertheless, not as I will, but as thou *wilt*.

40 And he cometh unto the disciples, and findeth them asleep, and saith unto Peter, What, could ye not watch with me one hour?

41 Watch and pray, that ye enter not into temptation: the spirit indeed *is* willing, but the flesh *is* weak.

42 He went away again the second time, and prayed, saying, O my Father, if this cup may not pass away from me, except I drink it, thy will be done.

43 And he came and found them asleep again: for their eyes were heavy.

44 And he left them, and went away again, and prayed the third time, saying the same words.

就帶了彼得和西庇太的兩個兒子去、耶穌便憂愁傷起心來對他們說、我心裏甚是憂傷幾乎要死你們在這裏等候和我一同儆醒、就往前行了幾步俯伏在地、祈禱說我父假若可行、就叫這一杯離開我、然而不要照著我的意思只要照著你的意回到門徒那裏見他們睡覺就對彼得說你不能同我儆醒片時麼、應當儆醒祈禱免得入了迷惑心裏固然願意身子却軟弱了耶穌又去第二次禱告說、我父、這一杯若不能離開我必要我喝就願你的意旨成全、囘來又看見他們睡覺因為他們眼睛困倦了、又離開他們去第二次禱告話也和先前一樣。

114 ST. MATTHEW.

45 Then cometh he to his disciples, and saith unto them, Sleep on now, and take *your* rest: behold, the hour is at hand, and the Son of man is betrayed into the hands of sinners.

46 Rise, let us be going: behold, he is at hand that doth betray me.

47 ¶ And while he yet spake, lo, Judas, one of the twelve, came, and with him a great multitude with swords and staves, from the chief priests and elders of the people.

48 Now he that betrayed him gave them a sign, saying, Whomsoever I shall kiss, that same is he; hold him fast.

49 And forthwith he came to Jesus, and said, Hail, Master; and kissed him.

50 And Jesus said unto him, Friend, wherefore art thou come? Then came they, and laid hands on Jesus, and took him.

51 And, behold, one of them which were with Jesus stretched out *his* hand, and drew his sword, and struck a servant of the high priest, and smote off his ear.

52 Then said Jesus unto him, Put up again the sword into his place: for all they that take the sword shall perish with the sword.

馬太第二十六章

後又囘到門徒那裏對他們說現在你們仍然睡覺安息罷時候到了人子被賣在罪人手裏了。起來、我們去罷、賣我的人離這裏不遠了。○說話之間、十二門徒裏的猶大帶著許多人拏著刀棒、從祭司長和民間的長老那裏來、賣耶穌的猶大趕緊到耶穌面前來說、請夫子安就和他親嘴耶穌對他說、明友你是為甚麼來的那些人就上前下手拏住耶穌跟從耶穌的一個人、伸手拔刀、砍大祭司的僕人削掉了他一耳朶。耶穌說收你的刀入鞘凡動刀的、必被刀所殺。

ST. MATTHEW.

53 Thinkest thou that I cannot now pray to my Father, and he shall presently give me more than twelve legions of angels?

54 But how then shall the Scriptures be fulfilled, that thus it must be?

55 In that same hour said Jesus to the multitudes, Are ye come out as against a thief with swords and staves for to take me? I sat daily with you teaching in the temple, and ye laid no hold on me.

56 But all this was done, that the Scriptures of the prophets might be fulfilled. Then all the disciples forsook him, and fled.

57 ¶ And they that had laid hold on Jesus led *him* to Caiaphas the high priest, where the scribes and the elders were assembled.

58 But Peter followed him afar off unto the high priest's palace, and went in, and sat with the servants, to see the end.

59 Now the chief priests, and elders, and all the council, sought false witness against Jesus, to put him to death;

60 But found none: yea, though many false witnesses came, *yet* found they none. At the last came two false witnesses,

馬太第二十六章

你想我現在不能求我天父、爲我差遣十二萬多天使下來麽。若是這樣、經上所說這事必有的那話怎能應驗呢。當時耶穌對衆人說你們帶著刀棒來捉我、如同捉賊麼我日日坐在殿裏教訓人、和你們在一處你們反倒不拏我、但這事成了爲要應驗先知所記的話這時候衆門徒都離開耶穌逃走了。○拏耶穌的人將耶穌解到大祭司該亞法那裏去、讀書人和長老都在那裏聚會彼得遠遠的跟隨耶穌、到了大祭司的院進入裏面和差役同坐要看這事的結局衆祭司長和長老並全公會的人尋找作假見證的控告耶穌要治死他只是尋不著證據雖有許多作假見證的人來、總得不著證據後來有兩個作假見證的人來說、

61 And said, This *fellow* said, I am able to destroy the temple of God, and to build it in three days.

62 And the high priest arose, and said unto him, Answerest thou nothing? what *is it which* these witness against thee?

63 But Jesus held his peace. And the high priest answered and said unto him, I adjure thee by the living God, that thou tell us whether thou be the Christ, the Son of God.

64 Jesus saith unto him, Thou hast said: nevertheless I say unto you, Hereafter shall ye see the Son of man sitting on the right hand of power, and coming in the clouds of heaven.

65 Then the high priest rent his clothes, saying, He hath spoken blasphemy; what further need have we of witnesses? behold, now ye have heard his blasphemy.

66 What think ye? They answered and said, He is guilty of death.

67 Then did they spit in his face, and buffeted him; and others smote *him* with the palms of their hands,

68 Saying, Prophesy unto us, thou Christ, Who is he that smote thee?

這個人曾說我能拆毀　神的殿、三日之內又建造起來。大祭司就起來、問耶穌說、你沒有話答對麼他們作見證告你的是甚麼。耶穌不作聲、大祭司又對他說我叫你在永生　神面前起誓告訴我你果然是　神的子基督不是。耶穌說你說的是了、只是我告訴你們後來你們要看見人子坐在有大權柄的主的右邊、駕著天上的雲降臨。大祭司就撕開自己的衣裳說他說僭妄的話了、何用別的見證現在你們都聽見他僭妄的話了。你們的意思如何、眾人囘答說他犯了死罪了、就吐唾沫在他臉上用拳頭打他、也有用手掌打他的說基督你是先知、可以告訴我說打你的是誰。

St. MATTHEW.

69 ¶ Now Peter sat without in the palace: and a damsel came unto him, saying, Thou also wast with Jesus of Galilee.

70 But he denied before *them* all, saying, I know not what thou sayest.

71 And when he was gone out into the porch, another *maid* saw him, and said unto them that were there, This *fellow* was also with Jesus of Nazareth.

72 And again he denied with an oath, I do not know the man.

73 And after a while came unto *him* they that stood by, and said to Peter, Surely thou also art *one* of them; for thy speech bewrayeth thee.

74 Then began he to curse and to swear, *saying*, I know not the man. And immediately the cock crew.

75 And Peter remembered the word of Jesus, which said unto him, Before the cock crow, thou shalt deny me thrice. And he went out, and wept bitterly.

○彼得坐在外院子裏、有一個使女進前來說、你也是跟從加利利耶穌的罷。彼得在衆人面前不認對他說你所說的我不知道就出來、到了門口又有一個使女看見他就對那裏的人說他也是跟從拏撒勒耶穌的人彼得又不認並且起誓說、我不認得這個人。過了不多的時候、旁邊站著的人進前來對彼得說你實在是他一黨的人、聽你的口音就是憑據了。彼得就發咒起誓的說我不認得這個人、立時雞就叫了。彼得想起耶穌對他所說雞叫之先你要三次說不認得我的話、就出去悲慘慘的哭起來了。

CHAPTER 27.

WHEN the morning was come, all the chief priests and elders of the people took counsel against Jesus to put him to death:

2 And when they had bound him, they led *him* away, and delivered him to Pontius Pilate the governor.

3 ¶ Then Judas, which had betrayed him, when he saw that he was condemned, repented himself, and brought again the thirty pieces of silver to the chief priests and elders,

4 Saying, I have sinned in that I have betrayed the innocent blood. And they said, What *is that* to us? see thou *to that.*

5 And he cast down the pieces of silver in the temple, and departed, and went and hanged himself.

6 And the chief priests took the silver pieces, and said, It is not lawful for to put them into the treasury, because it is the price of blood.

7 And they took counsel, and bought with them the potter's field, to bury strangers in.

第二十七章

「第二日早晨衆祭司長和民間的長老大家商議、要治死耶穌就將他綁上解往方伯本丟彼拉多那裏去。○這時候賣耶穌的猶大、看見耶穌被他們定了罪、就後悔、將三十塊銀錢還了祭司長和長老說我賣了無辜的人的性命是有罪了。他們說、這與我們甚麼相干、你自己承當罷猶大就將銀子丟在殿裏出去自縊死了。衆祭司長拾起銀子來、說這是賣性命的價銀、不可放在庫裏就彼此商議用這銀子買了燒窰的人的一塊田地作了埋藏外鄉人的義地。

ST. MATTHEW.

8 Wherefore that field was called, The field of blood, unto this day.
9 Then was fulfilled that which was spoken by Jeremy the prophet, saying, And they took the thirty pieces of silver, the price of him that was valued, whom they of the children of Israel did value;
10 And gave them for the potter's field, as the Lord appointed me.
11 And Jesus stood before the governor: and the governor asked him, saying, Art thou the King of the Jews? And Jesus said unto him, Thou sayest.
12 And when he was accused of the chief priests and elders, he answered nothing.
13 Then said Pilate unto him, Hearest thou not how many things they witness against thee?
14 And he answered him to never a word; insomuch that the governor marvelled greatly.
15 Now at *that* feast the governor was wont to release unto the people a prisoner, when they would.
16 And they had then a notable prisoner, called Barabbas.
17 Therefore when they were gathered together, Pilate said unto them, Whom will ye that I release unto you? Barabbas, or Jesus which is called Christ?

所以到如今這塊田還叫作血田就應了先知耶利米的話說、他們將這三十塊銀錢、就是以色列人所估定被賣的人的價銀買了燒窰的人的田地、這都是照著主所吩咐我的。○耶穌站在方伯面前、方伯問他說、你是猶太人的王麼、耶穌說你說的是。當下衆祭司長和長老告他、他都不回答。彼拉多就對他說這些人作見證告你這許多的事、你沒有聽見麼。耶穌還是不答一言方伯甚以爲奇。每到這個節方伯的規矩照衆人所要的釋放一個囚犯。那時候有一個出名的罪人叫作巴拉巴、衆人聚會的時候、彼拉多就問他們說你們要我釋放誰、是巴拉巴還是稱爲基督的耶穌呢。

ST. MATTHEW.

18 For he knew that for envy they had delivered him.

19 ¶ When he was set down on the judgment seat, his wife sent unto him, saying, Have thou nothing to do with that just man: for I have suffered many things this day in a dream because of him.

20 But the chief priests and elders persuaded the multitude that they should ask Barabbas, and destroy Jesus.

21 The governor answered and said unto them, Whether of the twain will ye that I release unto you? They said, Barabbas.

22 Pilate saith unto them, What shall I do then with Jesus which is called Christ? *They* all say unto him, Let him be crucified.

23 And the governor said, Why, what evil hath he done? But they cried out the more, saying, Let him be crucified.

24 ¶ When Pilate saw that he could prevail nothing, but *that* rather a tumult was made, he took water, and washed *his* hands before the multitude, saying, I am innocent of the blood of this just person: see ye *to it*.

25 Then answered all the people, and said, His blood *be* on us, and on our children.

26 ¶ Then released he Barabbas unto them: and when he had scourged Jesus, he delivered *him* to be crucified.

馬太第二十七章

彼拉多說這話、因為知道眾人媢妒耶穌、纔將他解了來坐堂的時候、彼拉多的妻子遣人對他說這義人的事你不可辦理因為我今日在夢裏多多的為他傷心祭司長和長老挑唆眾人、求放了巴拉巴、殺了耶穌、方伯對眾人說這兩個人你們要我放誰眾人說巴拉巴、彼拉多說那稱為基督的耶穌我怎樣辦法呢眾人都說釘在十字架上方伯說他作了甚麽惡事了、眾人越發喊叫說釘在十字架上、彼拉多見說也無益又恐怕生亂就在眾人面前拏水洗手說殺這義人不是我的罪你們自己承當罷眾百姓回答說殺他的罪都歸在我們和我們子孫身上於是彼拉多放了巴拉巴將耶穌鞭打了交給人釘他在十字架上。

ST. MATTHEW.

27 Then the soldiers of the governor took Jesus into the common hall, and gathered unto him the whole band *of soldiers*.

28 And they stripped him, and put on him a scarlet robe.

29 ¶ And when they had platted a crown of thorns, they put *it* upon his head, and a reed in his right hand: and they bowed the knee before him, and mocked him, saying, Hail, King of the Jews!

30 And they spit upon him, and took the reed, and smote him on the head.

31 And after that they had mocked him, they took the robe off from him, and put his own raiment on him, and led him away to crucify *him*.

32 And as they came out, they found a man of Cyrene, Simon by name: him they compelled to bear his cross.

33 And when they were come unto a place called Golgotha, that is to say, a place of a skull,

34 ¶ They gave him vinegar to drink mingled with gall: and when he had tasted *thereof*, he would not drink.

35 And they crucified him, and parted his garments, casting lots: that it might be fulfilled which was spoken by the prophet, They parted my garments among them, and upon my vesture did they cast lots.

馬太第二十七章

方伯的兵丁領耶穌進了公堂聚齊了全營的兵圍繞耶穌脫了耶穌的衣服給他穿上絳色袍用枳棘編作冕戴在他頭上拏一根葦子放在他右手裏跪在他面前戲弄他說請猶太人的王安就吐唾沫在他身上拏葦子打他的頭戲弄完了給他脫了袍穿了原舊的衣服拉他去要釘在十字架上出來的時候遇見一個古利奈人名叫西門就勉强他背著耶穌的十字架○到了一個地方叫作各各他繙出來就是髑髅地方用酢調和苦草汁給耶穌喝耶穌嘗了不肯喝他們將他釘在十字架上拈鬮分他的衣服正應了先知所說的話說他們分了我的外衣拈鬮分了我的裏衣。

ST. MATTHEW.

36 And sitting down they watched him there;

37 And set up over his head his accusation written, THIS IS JESUS THE KING OF THE JEWS.

38 Then were there two thieves crucified with him; one on the right hand, and another on the left.

39 ¶ And they that passed by reviled him, wagging their heads,

40 And saying, Thou that destroyest the temple, and buildest *it* in three days, save thyself. If thou be the Son of God, come down from the cross.

41 Likewise also the chief priests mocking *him*, with the scribes and elders, said,

42 He saved others; himself he cannot save. If he be the King of Israel, let him now come down from the cross, and we will believe him.

43 He trusted in God; let him deliver him now, if he will have him: for he said, I am the Son of God.

44 The thieves also, which were crucified with him, cast the same in his teeth.

45 Now from the sixth hour there was darkness over all the land unto the ninth hour,

馬太第二十七章

三六 眾兵丁坐在那裏看守他。

三七 又在他的頭以上、安一個牌、上面寫著告他的話、說這是猶太人的王耶穌。

三八 又有兩個強盜和他一同被釘十字架、一個在左邊、一個在右邊。○

三九 從那裏經過的人譏誚耶穌、搖頭說、

四十 拆毀聖殿三日又建造起來的、現在你救救自己罷、你果然是 神的兒子可以從十字架上下來。

四一 眾祭司長讀書人和長老、也戲弄他說他救別人倒不能救自己、他果然是以色列的王、可以從十字架上下來我們就信他、他是倚靠 神的、 神若喜悅他就必救他、因為他曾說我是 神的兒子那一同被釘的強盜、也是這樣的罵他。○

四二 從午正到申初、徧地都黑暗了。

ST. MATTHEW.

46 And about the ninth hour Jesus cried with a loud voice, saying, Eli, Eli, lama sabachthani? that is to say, My God, my God, why hast thou forsaken me?

47 Some of them that stood there, when they heard *that*, said, This *man* calleth for Elias.

48 And straightway one of them ran, and took a sponge, and filled *it* with vinegar, and put *it* on a reed, and gave him to drink.

49 The rest said, Let be, let us see whether Elias will come to save him.

50 ¶ Jesus, when he had cried again with a loud voice, yielded up the ghost.

51 And, behold, the vail of the temple was rent in twain from the top to the bottom; and the earth did quake, and the rocks rent;

52 And the graves were opened; and many bodies of the saints which slept arose,

53 And came out of the graves after his resurrection, and went into the holy city, and appeared unto many.

54 Now when the centurion, and they that were with him, watching Jesus, saw the earthquake, and those things that were done, they feared greatly, saying, Truly this was the Son of God.

馬太第二十七章

四六耶穌約在申初、大聲喊叫說以利、以利拉馬撒巴各大尼、就是說我 神、我 神、為甚麼離了我。旁邊站著的人聽見、有的說他叫以利亞呢他們裏頭有一個人就跑過來、拏海絨浸在醋裏綁在葦子上送給他喝。其餘的人說、且等著看以利亞來救他不來救他。○耶穌又大聲喊叫氣就絕了。忽然殿裏的幔子從上到下、裂為兩半、地震磐石崩裂、墳墓自開裏面去世原文作睡著的聖人的身體、多有起來的、到耶穌復活之後出了墳墓進了聖京被許多人看見百夫長和看守耶穌的人看見地動和那所經歷的事、就懼怕得很說這真是 神的兒子了。

124 ST. MATTHEW.

55 And many women were there beholding afar off, which followed Jesus from Galilee, ministering unto him:

56 Among which was Mary Magdalene, and Mary the mother of James and Joses, and the mother of Zebedee's children.

57 When the even was come, there came a rich man of Arimathea, named Joseph, who also himself was Jesus' disciple.

58 He went to Pilate, and begged the body of Jesus. Then Pilate commanded the body to be delivered.

59 And when Joseph had taken the body, he wrapped it in a clean linen cloth.

60 And laid it in his own new tomb, which he had hewn out in the rock: and he rolled a great stone to the door of the sepulchre, and departed.

61 And there was Mary Magdalene, and the other Mary, sitting over against the sepulchre.

62 ¶ Now the next day, that followed the day of the preparation, the chief priests and Pharisees came together unto Pilate,

63 Saying, Sir, we remember that that deceiver said, while he was yet alive, After three days I will rise again.

馬太第二十七章

有許多從加利利和耶穌同來、事奉耶穌的婦人、在那裏遠遠的觀看、內中有抹大拉的馬利亞、又有雅各和約西的母親馬利亞、並西庇太兩個兒子的母親、有一個財主、是亞利馬太的人、名叫約瑟、他也是耶穌的門徒、晚上到彼拉多那裏、求耶穌的身體、彼拉多就吩咐人將身體給他、約瑟取了身體用乾淨細蔴布裹起來、安放在自己的新墳墓裏這墳墓鑿在磐石之內、將大石轉在墓門口、就去了、有抹大拉的馬利亞和那個馬利亞對著墳墓坐在那裏、○次日就是豫備安息日的第二日、衆祭司長和法利賽人聚集來見彼拉多說大人、我們記得那引誘人的活著時候、曾說、三日後我要復活、

ST. MATTHEW.

64 Command therefore that the sepulchre be made sure until the third day, lest his disciples come by night, and steal him away, and say unto the people, He is risen from the dead: so the last error shall be worse than the first.

65 Pilate said unto them, Ye have a watch: go your way, make *it* as sure as ye can.

66 So they went, and made the sepulchre sure, sealing the stone, and setting a watch.

CHAPTER 28.

IN the end of the sabbath, as it began to dawn toward the first *day* of the week, came Mary Magdalene, and the other Mary to see the sepulchre.

2 And, behold, there was a great earthquake: for the angel of the Lord descended from heaven, and came and rolled back the stone from the door, and sat upon it.

3 His countenance was like lightning, and his raiment white as snow:

4 And for fear of him the keepers did shake, and became as dead *men*.

馬太第二十八章

現在請派人將他的墳墓看守三日、恐怕他徒弟夜間來、偷了他的身體去、後來告訴百姓說他是從死裏復活這樣那後來的迷惑比以前的更大了。彼拉多說你們自己有看守的兵、可以照著你們自己的意思去看守他們就去將墓門口的石頭封上了、派兵看守。

第二十八章

安息日既過七日的頭一日、天將亮的時候抹大拉的馬利亞、和那個馬利亞來看墳墓忽然地大震動主的使者從天降下進前將墓門口的石頭轉開坐在上邊他的像貌如同閃電、衣服潔白像雪看守墳墓的人懼怕、戰戰兢兢幾乎嚇死。

126 ST. MATTHEW.

5 And the angel answered and said unto the women, Fear not ye: for I know that ye seek Jesus, which was crucified.

6 He is not here: for he is risen, as he said. Come, see the place where the Lord lay.

7 And go quickly, and tell his disciples that he is risen from the dead; and, behold he goeth before you into Galilee; there shall ye see him: lo, I have told you.

8 And they departed quickly from the sepulchre with fear and great joy; and did run to bring his disciples word.

9 ¶ And as they went to tell his disciples, behold, Jesus met them, saying, All hail. And they came and held him by the feet, and worshipped him.

10 Then said Jesus unto them, Be not afraid: go tell my brethren that they go into Galilee, and there shall they see me.

11 ¶ Now when they were going, behold, some of the watch came into the city, and shewed unto the chief priests all the things that were done.

12 And when they were assembled with the elders, and had taken counsel, they gave large money unto the soldiers,

13 Saying, Say ye, His disciples came by night, and stole him *away* while we slept.

馬太第二十八章

天使對婦人說、不要懼怕、我知道你們尋找釘在十字架上的耶穌、他不在這裏、照著他所說的已經復活了、你且來看主葬埋的地方、快去告訴他的門徒說、他從死裏復活、要在你們以先往加利利去、在那裏可以見他、這話我告訴你們了。婦人就急忙從墳墓裏出來、又懼怕又大大的歡喜跑去報給耶穌的門徒知道。報去的時候、耶穌遇見他們、說、願你們平安、他們就上前抱住他的脚拜他、耶穌對他們說、不要懼怕、去告訴我弟兄往加利利去、在那裏可以見我。○婦人去後、有看守墳墓的人進城、將所經歷的事都報給眾祭司長。眾祭司長和長老聚集商議、拿許多銀子給兵丁、說、你們就說、我們夜間睡覺的時候、他的門徒來偷了他的身體去了。

14 And if this come to the governor's ears, we will persuade him, and secure you.

15 So they took the money, and did as they were taught: and this saying is commonly reported among the Jews until this day.

16 ¶ Then the eleven disciples went away into Galilee, into a mountain where Jesus had appointed them.

17 And when they saw him, they worshipped him: but some doubted.

18 And Jesus came and spake unto them, saying, All power is given unto me in heaven and in earth.

19 ¶ Go ye therefore, and teach all nations, baptizing them in the name of the Father, and of the Son, and of the Holy Ghost:

20 Teaching them to observe all things whatsoever I have commanded you: and, lo, I am with you alway *even* unto the end of the world. Amen.

倘若這話被方伯聽見、有我們勸他、保你們無事便了、兵丁受了銀子、照著那些人所囑咐他們的話去說、所以這話傳在猶太人中間直到如今〇十一個門徒往加利利去、到了耶穌所說的山上、看見耶穌、就拜他、然而還有人疑惑、耶穌進前對他們說、天上地上所有的權柄、都賜與我了、你們當去勸化萬民、作我的門徒、奉父子聖靈的名、給他們施洗、凡我所吩咐你們的、都教訓他們遵守、我就常在你們中間、直到世界的末日阿們。

www.ingramcontent.com/pod-product-compliance
Lightning Source LLC
Chambersburg PA
CBHW020109170426
43199CB00009B/465